High Output Management

High Output Management

◇

Andrew S. Grove

Random House . *New York*

Library of Congress Cataloging in Publication Data
Grove, Andrew S.
High output management.
Includes index.
1. Industrial management. I. Title.
HD31.G764 1983 658.5 83-3412
ISBN 0-394-53234-1

Manufactured in the United States of America

2 4 6 8 9 7 5 3

First Edition

Acknowledgments

The ideas in this book are the result of a collective effort —my collaboration with many, many Intel managers over the years. I am very grateful to all of them, because I learned everything I know about how to manage from them. I am especially grateful to Gordon Moore, one of the founders of Intel, who recognized the budding manager under my engineer's skin long before I had any inkling myself.

Thanks are also due to a group of the company's middle managers who cheerfully accepted the role of guinea pig, who suffered through my first attempts to articulate these ideas, and who also generously provided me with experiences from their daily lives as managers. I've used their examples to illustrate certain points in the book. These managers are acknowledged by name in the Notes.

I owe special thanks to Grant Ujifusa, my Random House editor, who tirelessly hammered away at the rough edges of my ideas and prose and translated the latter into English—from the original engineeringese; to Pam Johnson, who ran the various revisions through the word processor; and most of all to Charlene King, my assistant, who not only helped to pull the whole project together, from capturing class discussions to gathering illustrations, but also made sure that I did my work of running Intel even as I was busily splitting infinitives.

Contents

Introduction

Let me begin by telling you what this book is not about. There's not a sentence in it about bits and bytes, RAMs and ROMs, or anything else remotely technical or arcane, even though Intel, where I work, is a "high-tech," Silicon Valley company. As a practitioner of the art of management, I've tried instead to lay out what I think constitutes a good, solid management approach. From my experience at Intel, this consists of energetic and committed people sitting down together, looking at problems, and figuring out ways to solve them. So my job in the book is to provide you with basic ideas, clear principles, and specific techniques you can *use* in your own managerial circumstances.

I am especially eager to reach the middle manager, the usually forgotten man or woman of any organization. The first-line supervisor on the shop floor and the chief executive officer of a company are both well appreciated. You'll find many courses designed to teach the former the fundamentals of his work, while practically all of our leading business schools are set up to turn out the latter. But between the two is a large group of people, the middle managers, who supervise the shop-floor foreman, or who work as engineers, accountants, and sales representatives. Middle managers are the muscle and bone of every sizable organization, but they are largely ignored despite their immense importance to our society and economy.

Middle managers are not confined to big corporations. In fact, they can be found in almost any business operation. If you run a small tax department at a law firm, you are a middle manager. The same is true if you are a school principal, an owner of a distributorship, or a small-town insurance agent. When people from each of these enterprises read the manuscript, their reactions confirmed what I suspected: the broad applicability of the managerial ideas that were developed at Intel as it grew from a very small to a very large organization.

Another group should be included among middle managers—people who may not supervise anyone directly but who even without strict organizational authority affect and influence the work of others. These *know-how managers* are sources of knowledge, skills, and understanding to people around them in an organization. They are specialists and experts of some sort who act like consultants to other members of the organization. Teachers, market researchers, computer mavens, and traffic engineers shape the work of others through their know-how just as much as or more than the traditional manager using supervisory authority. Thus a know-how manager can be legitimately called a middle manager. In fact, the more our world becomes information- and service-oriented, the more importance know-how managers will acquire as members of middle management. In short, know-how managers should read on.

At various times you will take exception to what you read. "This may be fine at Intel," you will say, "but it would never fly at PDQ, where I work. Nothing does until the Old Man himself decrees it. Short of a palace revolution, I can't use anything you recommend." Let me assure you that you *will* be able to use most of what I say. As a middle manager, of any sort, you are in effect a chief executive of an organization yourself. Don't wait for the principles and the practices you find appealing or valid to be imposed from the top. As a *micro CEO*, you can X improve your own and your group's performance and productivity, whether or not the rest of the company follows suit.

The book contains three basic ideas. The first is an output-oriented approach to management. That is to say, we apply some of the principles and the discipline of the most output-oriented of endeavors—*manufacturing*—to other forms of business enterprise, including most emphatically the work of managers. Consider Intel, which is a true manufacturing and production company, making highly complex silicon chips as well as computer-like products built from them. Our company now has about 20,000 employees. Of these, 8,000 actually work to make the products. Another 3,000 help them, as they supervise the personnel, maintain the machines, engineer, and improve the manufacturing process. Another 5,000 work in administration, where they schedule production, keep personnel records, send bills to our customers, and pay our suppliers. Finally, some 4,000 design new products, take them to the marketplace, sell them, and service them after the sale.

As we founded, organized, and managed Intel, we found that *all* our employees "produce" in some sense —some make chips, others prepare bills, while still others create software designs or advertising copy. We also found that when we approached any work done at Intel with this basic understanding in mind, the principles and discipline of production gave us a systematic way of managing it, much as the language and concepts of finance created a common approach to evaluating and managing investments of any sort.

The second idea is that the work of a business, of a government bureaucracy, of most forms of human activity, is something pursued not by individuals but by teams. This idea is summed up in what I regard as the single most important sentence of this book: The output of a manager *is* the output of the organizational units under his supervision or influence. The question then becomes what can managers do to increase the output of their teams. Put another way, what specifically should they be doing during the day when a virtually limitless number of possible tasks calls for their attention? To give you a way to answer the question, I introduce the concept of *managerial leverage,* which measures the impact of what managers do to increase the output of their teams. High managerial productivity, I argue, depends largely on choosing to perform tasks that possess high leverage.

A team will perform well only if peak performance is elicited from the individuals in it. This is the third idea of the book. Can business use whatever it is that motivates an athlete to put out his "personal best" consistently? I think business can, which is why I examine the *sports analogy* and the role of something called task-relevant feedback to get and to sustain a high level of performance from the members of a business team.

I am an engineer by training and a manager of a high-technology company by profession. As a manager, I am also a member of that group—many millions strong just in the United States—which holds the key to increased productivity: more and better goods and services to meet people's needs. I am an optimist and believe our potential to increase our wealth has hardly been tapped. I also strongly believe that applying the methods of *production,* exercising *managerial leverage,* and eliciting an athlete's desire for peak *performance* can help nearly everyone— lawyers, teachers, engineers, supervisors, even book editors; in short, middle managers of all kinds—to work more productively.

So, let us begin by taking a field trip to a factory . . .

Part One

THE
BREAKFAST
FACTORY

1
The Basics of Production: Delivering a Breakfast
(or a College Graduate,
or a Compiler, or a
Convicted Criminal . . .)

The Three-Minute Egg

To understand the principles of production, imagine that you're a waiter, which I was while I went to college, and that your task is to serve a breakfast consisting of a three-minute soft-boiled egg, buttered toast, and coffee. Your job is to prepare and deliver the three items simultaneously, each of them fresh and hot.

The task here encompasses the basic requirements of production. These are to build and deliver products in response to the demands of the customer at a *scheduled* delivery time, at an *acceptable* quality level, and at the *lowest* possible cost. Production's charter cannot be to deliver whatever the customer wants whenever he wants it, for this would require an infinite production capacity or the equivalent—very large, ready-to-deliver inventories. In our example, the customer may want to have a perfect three-minute egg with hot buttered toast and steaming coffee waiting for him the moment he sits down. To fulfill such an expectation, you would either have to have your kitchen idle and poised to serve the customer whenever he drops in, or have a ready-to-consume inventory of perfectly boiled eggs, hot buttered toast, and coffee. Neither is practical.

Instead, a manufacturer should accept the responsibility of delivering a product at the time committed to —in this case, by implication, about five to ten minutes after the customer arrives at our breakfast establishment. And we must make our breakfast at a cost that enables us to sell it at a competitive price and still make an acceptable profit. How are we going to do this in the most intelligent way? We start by looking at our production flow.

The first thing we must do is to pin down the step in the flow that will determine the overall shape of our operation, which we'll call the *limiting step*. The issue here is simple: which of the breakfast components takes the longest to prepare? Because the coffee is already steaming in the kitchen and the toast takes only about a minute, the answer is obviously the egg, so we should plan the entire job around the time needed to boil it. Not only does that component take the longest to prepare, the egg is also for most customers the most important feature of the breakfast.

What must happen is illustrated opposite. To work back from the time of delivery, you'll need to calculate the time required to prepare the three components to ensure that they are all ready simultaneously. First you must allow time to assemble the items on a tray. Next you must get the toast from the toaster and the coffee from the pot, as well as the egg out of the boiling water. Adding the required time to do this to the time needed to get and cook the egg defines the length of the entire process—called, in production jargon, the total throughput time.

Now you come to the toast. Using the egg time as your base, you must allow yourself time to get and toast the slices of bread. Finally, using the toast time as your base, you can determine when you need to pour the coffee. The

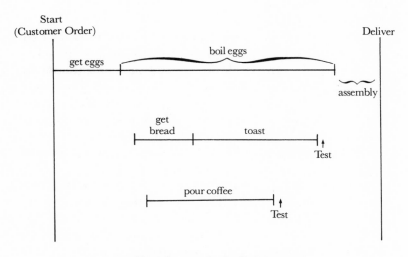

Making the eggs is the limiting step.

key idea is that we construct our production flow by starting with the longest (or most difficult, or most sensitive, or most expensive) step and work our way back. Notice when each of the three steps began and ended. We planned our flow around the most critical step—the time required to boil the egg—and we staggered each of the other steps according to individual throughput times; again in production jargon, we *offset* them from each other.

The idea of a limiting step has very broad applicability. Take, for example, the need to recruit college graduates to work for Intel. Certain of our managers visit the colleges, interview some of the seniors, and invite the more promising candidates to visit the company. We bear the expense of the candidates' trip, which can be considerable. During the trip, the students are closely interviewed by other managers and technical people. After due consideration, employment is offered to some of the students whose skills and capabilities match our needs best, and those who accept the offers eventually come to work for the company.

To apply the basic principle of production, you need to build the sequence here around its most expensive feature, which is the students' trip to the plant, thanks to the cost of travel and the time that Intel managers spend with the candidates. To minimize the use of this step per final college hire, we obviously have to increase the ratio of accepted offers to applicants invited to visit the plant, which we do by using phone interviews to screen people before issuing invitations. The technique saves money, substantially increases the ratio of offers extended per plant visit, and reduces the need to use the expensive limiting step per hire.

The principle of time offsets is also present here. Working back from the time the students will graduate, the recruiter staggers the various steps involved to allow time for everything—on-campus interviews, phone screening, plant visits—to take place at the appropriate times during the months preceding graduation.

Production Operations

Other production principles underlie the preparation of our breakfast. In the making of it, we find present the three fundamental types of production operations: *process* manufacturing, an activity that physically or chemically changes material just as boiling changes an egg; *assembly*, in which components are put together to constitute a new entity just as the egg, the toast, and the coffee together make a breakfast; and *test*, which subjects the components or the total to an examination of its characteristics. There are, for example, visual tests made at points in the breakfast production process: you can see that the coffee is steaming and that the toast is brown.

Process, assembly, and test operations can be readily

applied to other very different kinds of productive work. Take, for instance, the task of training a sales force to sell a new product. The three types of production operations can be easily identified. The conversion of large amounts of raw data about the product into meaningful selling strategies comprehensible to the sales personnel is a process step, which transforms data into strategies. The combination of the various sales strategies into a coherent program can be compared to an assembly step. Here the appropriate product-selling strategies and pertinent market data (such as competitive pricing and availability) are made to flow into one presentation, along with such things as brochures, handouts, and flip charts. The test operation comes in the form of a "dry run" presentation with a selected group of field sales personnel and field sales management. If the dry run fails the test, the material must be "reworked" (another well-established manufacturing concept) to meet the concerns and objections of the test audience.

The development of a "compiler," a major piece of computer software, also demonstrates process, assembly, and test. A computer understands and uses human instruction only if it receives such instruction in its own language. A compiler is an interpreter, enabling the computer to translate into its language material written in terms and phrases resembling English. With a compiler, a programmer can think more or less like a human being rather than having to adapt himself to the way the computer processes information. The task of getting a machine to interpret and translate in this fashion is obviously formidable; thus the development of a compiler takes strenuous effort on the part of skilled and gifted software engineers. The effort, however, is justified by the simplification it brings to computer use.

In any case, the development of the individual pieces out of which a compiler is built represents a series of processing steps. Actual working pieces of software are generated out of specifications and basic design know-how. Each piece then undergoes an individual operation called a "unit test." When one fails, the defective portion of the software is returned to the process phase for "re-work." After all the pieces pass their respective unit tests, they are assembled to form the compiler. Then, of course, a "system test" is performed on the complete product before it is shipped to the customer. Time off-sets are used extensively in the task. Because throughput times for the various engineering steps are well estab-lished, the timing of the releases of various bodies of software from one stage to another can all be calculated and staged in advance.

Breakfast preparation, college recruiting, sales train-ing, and compiler design are very much unlike one an-other, but all of them possess a basically similar flow of activity to produce a specific output.

A Few Complications

Real life, as you know, is full of thickets and underbrush. In a schematic flow chart, our breakfast operation as-sumed infinite capacity, meaning that nobody had to wait for an available toaster or for a pot to boil an egg in. But no such ideal world exists. What would happen if you had to stand in a line of waiters, waiting for your turn to use the toaster? If you didn't adjust your production flow to account for the queue, your three-minute egg could easily become a six-minute egg. So limited toaster capac-ity means you have to redo your flow around the new limiting step. The egg still determines the overall quality of the breakfast, but your time offsets must be altered.

How would our model reflect the change in manufac-turing flow? Working back from the time of breakfast delivery, let's see how the production is affected, as illus-trated opposite. The egg cycle remains the same, as does the one for coffee. But limited toaster capacity makes for quite a difference. Now you must account for the delivery time of the toast and the wait for a free toaster. This means the whole production process has to be conceived differently. Toaster capacity has become the limiting step, and what you do has to be reworked around it.

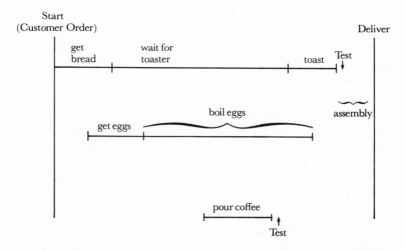

With limited toaster capacity, making the toast becomes the limiting step.

Now let's complicate things a little further. What happens if you are stuck in line waiting for a toaster when it's time to start boiling your egg? Your conflict is seemingly irreconcilable, but it really isn't. If you were managing the restaurant, you could turn your personnel into *specialists* by hiring one egg-cooker, one toast-maker, one coffee-pourer, and one person to supervise the operation. But that, of course, creates an immense amount of *overhead,* probably making it too expensive to consider.

If you were a waiter, you could ask the waiter in line next to you to help out—to put your toast in while you ran off to start your egg. But when you have to depend on someone else, the results are likely to be less predictable. As the manager, you could add another toaster, but this becomes an expensive addition of *capital equipment.* You could run the toaster continuously and build up an *inventory* of hot toast, throwing away what you can't use but always having immediate access to product. That means waste, which can also become too expensive for the operation. But at least you know that alternatives do exist: equipment capacity, manpower, and inventory can be traded off against each other and then balanced against delivery time.

Because each alternative costs money, your task is to find the *most cost-effective* way to deploy your resources— the key to optimizing all types of productive work. Bear in mind that in this and in other such situations there is a right answer, the one that can give you the best delivery time and product quality at the lowest possible cost. To find that right answer, you must develop a clear understanding of the trade-offs between the various factors— manpower, capacity, and inventory—and you must reduce the understanding to a quantifiable set of relationships. You probably won't use a stopwatch to conduct a time-and-motion study of the person behind a toaster; nor will you calculate the precise trade-off between the cost of toast inventory and the added toaster capacity in mathematical terms. What is important is the thinking you force yourself to go through to understand the relationship between the various aspects of your production process.

Let's take our manufacturing example a step further and turn our business into a high-volume breakfast factory operation. First, you buy a *continuous egg-boiler* that will produce a constant supply of perfectly boiled three-minute eggs. It will look something like what's drawn in the figure opposite. Note that our business now assumes a high and predictable demand for three-minute eggs; it cannot now readily provide a four-minute egg, because automated equipment is not very flexible. Second, you match the output of the continuous egg-boiler with the output of a continuous toaster, as specialized personnel load each piece of equipment and deliver the product. We have now turned things into a *continuous operation* at the expense of flexibility, and we can no longer prepare each customer's order exactly when and how he requests it. So our customers have to adjust their expectations if they want to enjoy the benefits of our new mode: lower cost and more predictable product quality.

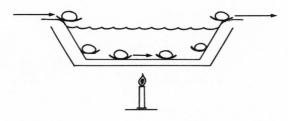

The continuous egg-boiler: a constant supply of three-minute eggs.

But continuous operation does not automatically mean lower cost and better quality. What would happen if the water temperature in the continuous egg-boiler quietly went out of specification? The entire work-in-process—all the eggs in the boiler—and the output of the machine from the time the temperature climbed or dropped to the time the malfunction was discovered becomes unusable. All the toast is also wasted because you don't have any eggs to serve with it. How do you minimize the risk of a breakdown of this sort? Performing a *functional test* is one way. From time to time you open an egg as it comes out of the machine and check its quality. But you will have to throw away the egg tested. A second way involves *in-process inspection,* which can take many forms. You could, for example, simply insert a thermometer into the water so that the temperature could be easily and frequently checked. To avoid having to pay someone to read the thermometer, you could connect an electronic gadget to it that would set off bells anytime the temperature varied by a degree or two. The point is that whenever possible, you should choose in-process tests over those that destroy product.

What else could go wrong with our continuous egg-machine? The eggs going into it could be cracked or rotten, or they could be over- or undersized, which would affect how fast they cook. To avoid such problems, you will want to look at the eggs at the time of receipt, something called *incoming* or *receiving inspection.* If the eggs are unacceptable in some way, you are going to have to send them back, leaving you with none. Now you have to shut down. To avoid that, you need a *raw material inventory.* But how large should it be? The principle to be applied here is that you should have enough to cover your consumption rate for the length of time it takes to replace your raw material. That means if your egg man comes by and delivers once a day, you want to keep a day's worth of inventory on hand to protect yourself. But remember, inventory costs money, so you have to weigh the advantage of carrying a day's supply against the cost of carrying it. Besides the cost of the raw material and the cost of money, you should also try to gauge the *opportunity at risk:* what would it cost if you had to shut your egg machine down for a day? How many customers would you lose? How much would it cost to lure them back? Such questions define the opportunity at risk.

Adding Value

All production flows have a basic characteristic: the material becomes more valuable as it moves through the process. A boiled egg is more valuable than a raw one, a fully assembled breakfast is more valuable than its constituent parts, and finally, the breakfast placed in front of the customer is more valuable still. The last carries the perceived value the customer associates with the establishment when he drives into the parking lot after seeing the sign "Andy's Better Breakfasts." Similarly, a finished compiler is more valuable than the constituent parts of semantic analysis, code generation, and run time, and a college graduate to whom we are ready to extend an employment offer is more valuable to us than the college student we meet on campus for the first time.

A common rule we should always try to heed is to detect and fix any problem in a production process at the *lowest-value* stage possible. Thus, we should find and reject the rotten egg as it's being delivered from our supplier rather than permitting the customer to find it. Likewise, if we can decide that we don't want a college candidate at the time of the campus interview rather than during the course of a plant visit, we save the cost of the trip and the time of both the candidate and the interviewers. And we should also try to find any performance problem at the time of the unit test of the pieces that make up a compiler rather than in the course of the test of the final product itself.

Finally, at the risk of being considered hard-hearted, let's examine the criminal justice system as if it were a production process aimed at finding criminals and putting them into jail. The production begins when a crime is reported to the police and the police respond. In many instances, after some questions are asked, no further action can be taken. For those crimes which the police can pursue, the second step is more investigation. But the case often ends here for lack of evidence, complaints being dropped, and so on. If things move to the next stage, a suspect is arrested, and the police try to find witnesses and build a case, hoping to get an indictment. Once again, an indictment is often not returned because of insufficient evidence. For the cases that actually do go ahead, the next stage is trial. Sometimes the suspect is found not guilty; sometimes the case is dismissed. But when a conviction is secured, the process moves to the sentencing and appeals round. At times a person found guilty of a crime will be given a suspended sentence and probation, and at others the conviction will be overturned on appeal. For the small fraction that remains, the final stage is jail.

If we make some reasoned assumptions about the percentages that move forward at each stage and the costs associated with each, we arrive at some striking conclusions. If we compile the cost of the effort that goes into securing a conviction and assign it only to those criminals who actually end up in jail, we find that the cost of a single conviction works out to be well over a million dollars—an absolutely staggering sum. The number is so high, of course, because only a very small percentage of the flow of accused persons makes it all the way through the process. Everyone knows that prisons are overcrowded, and that many criminals end up serving shorter jail terms or no jail terms at all because cells are in such short supply. So a terribly expensive trade-off results, violating the most important production principles. The limiting step here should clearly be obtaining a conviction. The construction cost of a jail cell even today is only some $80,000. This, plus the $10–20,000 it costs to keep a person in jail for a year, is a small amount compared to the million dollars required to secure a conviction. Not to jail a criminal in whom society has invested over a million dollars for lack of an $80,000 jail cell clearly misuses society's total investment in the criminal justice system. And this happens because we permit the wrong step (the availability of jail cells) to limit the overall process.

2
Managing the Breakfast Factory

Indicators as a Key Tool

A hungry public has loved the breakfast you've been serving, and thanks to the help of your many customers and a friendly banker, you've created a *breakfast factory,* which among other things uses specialized production lines for toast, coffee, and eggs. As manager of the factory, you have a substantial staff and a lot of automated equipment. But to run your operation well, you will need a set of good *indicators,* or *measurements.* Your output, of course, is no longer the breakfasts you deliver personally but rather all the breakfasts your factory delivers, profits generated, and the satisfaction of your customers. Just to get a fix on your output, you need a number of indicators; to get efficiency and high output, you need even more of them. The number of possible indicators you can choose is virtually limitless, but for any set of them to be useful, you have to *focus* each indicator on a specific operational goal.

Let's say that as manager of the breakfast factory, you will work with five indicators to meet your production goals on a daily basis. Which five would they be? Put another way, which five pieces of information would you want to look at each day, immediately upon arriving at your office?

Here are my candidates. First, you'll want to know your *sales forecast* for the day. How many breakfasts should you plan to deliver? To assess how much confidence you should place in your forecast, you would want to know how many you delivered yesterday compared to how many you planned on delivering—in other words, the *variance* between your plan and the actual delivery of breakfasts for the preceding day.

Your next key indicator is *raw material inventory*. Do you have enough eggs, bread, and coffee on hand to keep your factory running today? If you find you have too little inventory, you can still order more. If you find you have too much, you may want to cancel today's egg delivery.

Another important piece of information is the condition of your *equipment*. If anything broke down yesterday, you will want to get it repaired or rearrange your production line to meet your forecast for the day.

You also must get a fix on your *manpower*. If two waiters are out sick, you will have to come up with something if you are still going to meet the demand forecasted. Should you call in temporary help? Should you take someone off the toaster line and make him a waiter?

Finally, you want to have some kind of *quality* indicator. It is not enough to monitor the number of breakfasts each waiter delivers, because the waiters could have been rude to the customers even as they served a record number of breakfasts. Because your business depends on people wanting what you sell, you must be concerned with the public's opinion of your service. Perhaps you should set up a "customer complaint log" maintained by the cashier. If one of your waiters elicited more than the usual number of complaints yesterday, you will want to speak to him first thing today.

All these indicators measure factors essential to running your factory. If you look at them early every day, you will often be able to do something to correct a potential problem before it becomes a real one during the course of the day.

Indicators tend to direct your attention toward what they are monitoring. It is like riding a bicycle: you will probably steer it where you are looking. If, for example, you start measuring your inventory levels carefully, you are likely to take action to drive your inventory levels down, which is good up to a point. But your inventories could become so lean that you can't react to changes in demand without creating shortages. So because indicators direct one's activities, you should guard against overreacting. This you can do by *pairing* indicators, so that together both effect and counter-effect are measured. Thus, in the inventory example, you need to monitor both inventory levels and the incidence of shortages. A rise in the latter will obviously lead you to do things to keep inventories from becoming too low.

The principle here was evident many times in the development of a compiler. Measuring the completion date of each software unit against its capability is one example. Watching this pair of indicators should help us to avoid working on the perfect compiler that will never be ready, and also to avoid rushing to finish one that is inadequate. In sum, joint monitoring is likely to keep things in the optimum middle ground.

Nowhere can indicators—and paired indicators—be of more help than in administrative work. Having come to this realization, our company has been using measurements as a key tool to improve the productivity of administrative work for several years. The first rule is that a measurement—any measurement—is better than none. But a genuinely effective indicator will cover the *output* of the work unit and not simply the *activity* involved. Obviously, you measure a salesman by the orders he gets (output), not by the calls he makes (activity).

The second criterion for a good indicator is that what

you measure should be a *physical, countable* thing. Examples of effective measures of administrative output are shown below. Because those listed here are all quantity or output indicators, their paired counterparts should stress the *quality* of work. Thus, in accounts payable, the number of vouchers processed should be paired with the number of errors found either by auditing or by our suppliers. For another example, the number of square feet cleaned by a custodial group should be paired with a partially objective/partially subjective rating of the quality of work as assessed by a senior manager with an office in that building.

ADMINISTRATIVE FUNCTION	WORK OUTPUT INDICATOR
Accounts payable	# Vouchers processed
Custodial	# Square feet cleaned
Customer service	# Sales orders entered
Data entry	# Transactions processed
Employment	# People hired (by type of hire)
Inventory control	# Items managed in inventory

Examples of administrative work output indicators.

Such indicators have many uses. First, they spell out very clearly what the objectives of an individual or group are. Second, they provide a degree of objectivity when measuring an administrative function. Third, and as important as any, they give us a measure by which various administrative groups performing the same function in different organizations can be compared with each other. The performance of a custodial group in one major building can now be compared with that of another group in a second building. In fact, if indicators are put in place, the competitive spirit engendered frequently has an electrifying effect on the motivation each group brings to its work, along with a parallel improvement in performance. More about this later when we examine the "sports analogy."

The Black Box

We can think of our breakfast factory as if it were a "black box": input (the raw materials) and the labor of waiters, helpers, and you, the manager, flowing into the box, and the output (the breakfast) flowing out of it as illustrated below. In general, we can represent any activity that resembles a production process in a simple fashion as

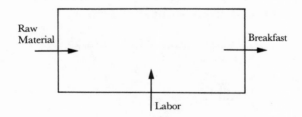

The breakfast factory—as a "black box."

a black box. Thus, we can draw a black box to represent college recruiting, where the input is the applicants on campus and the output is college graduates who have accepted our employment offers. The labor is the work of our on-campus interviewers and the managers and technical people who interview back at the plant. Similarly, the process of field sales training can be seen as a black box with the input being the raw product specifications and the output being trained sales personnel. The labor here is the work of the marketing and merchandising people who turn raw information into usable sales tools and train the field sales personnel to exploit them. In fact, we can represent most, if not all, administrative work by our magical black box. A group whose job is to bill customers has as its input the information about the customer—what he has purchased, the pricing data, and the shipment records; and output is the final bill sent to the customer through which payment is collected. The labor is the work of all personnel involved.

The black box sorts out what the inputs, the output, and the labor are in the production process. We can improve our ability to run that process by cutting some *windows* in our box so that we can see some of what goes on within it. By looking through the openings, as illustrated below, we can better understand the internal workings of any production process and assess what the future output is likely to be.

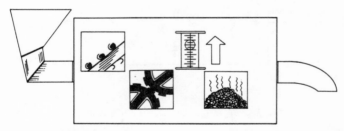

By peering through the windows in the black box, we can get an idea of what the future output is likely to be.

Leading indicators give you one way to look inside the black box by showing you in advance what the future might look like. And because they give you time to take corrective action, they make it possible for you to avoid problems. Of course, for leading indicators to do you any good, *you must believe in their validity.* While this may seem obvious, in practice, confidence is not as easy to come by as it sounds. To take big, costly, or worrisome steps when you are not yet sure you have a problem is hard. But unless you are prepared to act on what your leading indicators are telling you, all you will get from monitoring them is anxiety. Thus, the indicators you choose should be credible, so that you will, in fact, act whenever they flash warning signals.

Leading indicators might include the daily monitors we use to run our breakfast factory, from machine down-time records to an index of customer satisfaction—both of which can tell us if problems lie down the road. A generally applicable example of a "window" cut into the black box is the *linearity indicator.* In the figure below, we provide one for the college recruiting process. Plotted here is the number of college graduates who have accepted our offers versus the month of the year. If all went ideally, we would move along the straight line that would yield our hiring target for the semester by the month of June. If by April the actual progress is as shown here, we will find ourselves far below the ideal straight line. So

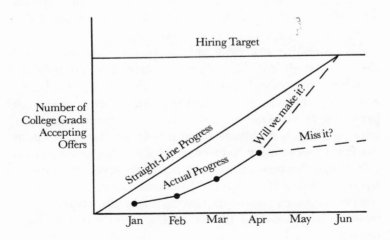

The linearity indicator can give us an early warning that we are likely to miss our target.

from reading the indicator, we know that the only way we can hit our target is by getting acceptance at a much higher rate in the remaining two months than we had gotten in the preceding four. Thus, the linearity indicator flashes an early warning, allowing us time to take corrective action. Without it, we would discover that we had missed our target in June, when nothing can be done about it.

If we consider a manufacturing unit in this fashion, we may assume that because it makes monthly goals regularly, all is well. But we can cut a window into the black box here, measure production output against time as the month proceeds, and compare that with the ideal linear output. We may learn that output performance is spread evenly throughout the course of the month or that it is concentrated in the last week of the month. If the latter is the case, the manager of the unit is probably not using manpower and equipment efficiently. And if the situation is not remedied, one minor breakdown toward month's end could cause the unit to miss its monthly output goal entirely. The linearity indicator will help you anticipate such a problem and is therefore quite valuable.

Also valuable are *trend indicators*. These show output (breakfasts delivered, software modules completed, vouchers processed) measured against time (performance this month versus performance over a series of previous months), and also against some standard or expected level. A display of trends forces you to look at the future as you are led to extrapolate almost automatically from the past. This extrapolation gives us another window in our black box. Also, measurement against a standard makes you think through *why* the results were what they were, and not what the standard said they would be.

Another sound way to anticipate the future is through the use of the *stagger chart,* which forecasts an output over the next several months. The chart is updated monthly, so that each month you will have an updated version of the then-current forecast information as compared to several prior forecasts. You can readily see the variation of one forecast from the next, which can help you anticipate future trends better than if you used a simple trend chart.

In my experience, nowhere has the stagger chart been more productive than in forecasting economic trends. The way it works is shown in the figure below, which gives us forecasted rates of incoming orders for an Intel division. The stagger chart then provides the same forecast prepared in the following month, in the month after that, and so on. Such a chart shows not only your outlook for business month by month but also how your outlook

Forecasted incoming orders for:

Forecast made in:	JUL	AUG	SEP	OCT	NOV	DEC	1982 JAN	FEB	MAR	APR	MAY	JUN
JUL '81	22	28	34	29								
AUG	*23	27	33	31	29							
SEP		*21	30	30	35	33						
OCT			*29	32	32	32	29					
NOV				*27	32	31	32	31				
DEC					*27	27	31	30	40			
JAN '82						*26	28	29	39	30		
FEB							*24	30	36	32	34	
MAR												

(* means the actual number for that month)

I have found the "stagger chart" the best means of getting a feel for future business trends.

varied from one month to the next. This way of looking at incoming business, of course, makes whoever does the forecasting take his task very seriously, because he knows that his forecast for any given month will be routinely compared with future forecasts and eventually with the actual result. But even more important, the improvement or deterioration of the forecasted outlook from one month to the next provides the most valuable indicator of business trends that I have ever seen. I would go as far as to say that it's too bad that all economists and investment advisers aren't obliged to display their forecasts in a stagger chart form. Then we could really have a way to evaluate whatever any one of them chooses to say.

Finally, indicators can be a big help in solving all types of problems. If something goes wrong, you will have a bank of information that readily shows all the parameters of your operation, allowing you to scan them for unhealthy departures from the norm. If you do not systematically collect and maintain an archive of indicators, you will have to do an awful lot of quick research to get the information you need, and by the time you have it, the problem is likely to have gotten worse.

Controlling Future Output

There are two ways to control the output of any factory. Some industries *build to order*. For example, when you go shopping for a sofa, you are going to have to wait a long time to get what you bought, unless you buy it right off the floor. A furniture factory builds to order. When it learns what you want, the factory looks for a hole in its manufacturing schedule and makes the item for you. If you order a new car rather than buying one right off the lot, the same thing happens: the plant will paint the car in the color you want and provide the options you want, but you will have to wait for it. And our breakfast factory, of course, builds breakfasts to order.

But if your competition in the sofa business makes the same product but has it ready in four weeks while you need four months, you are not going to have many customers. So even though you would much rather build to order, you will have to use another way to control the output of your factory. In short, you will have to *build to forecast*, which is a *contemplation of future orders*. To do this, the manufacturer sets up his activities around a reasoned speculation that orders will materialize for specific products within a certain time.

An obvious disadvantage here is that the manufacturer takes an inventory risk. Since the forecast is an assessment of future requirements, which the manufacturer commits resources to satisfy, the factory could be in an immense amount of trouble if the orders do not materialize or if they materialize for a product other than the one anticipated. In either case, unwanted inventory is the result. To build to forecast, you risk capital to respond to anticipated future demand in good order.

At Intel, we build to forecast because our customers demand that we respond to their needs in a timely fashion, even though our manufacturing throughput times are quite long. Our breakfast factory makes its product to customer order, but buys from its suppliers—like the egg man—on the basis of forecasted demand. Similarly, most companies recruit new college graduates to fill anticipated needs—rather than recruiting only when a need develops, which would be foolish because college graduates are turned out in a highly seasonal fashion. Computer software products, such as compilers, are also typically developed in response to an anticipated market need rather than to specific customer order. So "building" to forecast is a very common business practice.

Delivering a product that was built to forecast to a customer consists of two simultaneous processes, each with a separate time cycle. A manufacturing flow must occur in which the raw material moves through various production steps and finally enters the finished goods warehouse, as illustrated below. Simultaneously, a salesman finds a prospect and sells to that prospect, who eventually places an order with the manufacturer. Ideally, the order for the product and the product itself should arrive on the shipping dock at the same time.

Because the art and science of forecasting is so complex, you might be tempted to give all forecasting responsibility to a single manager who can be made accountable for it. But this usually does not work very well. What works better is to ask both the manufacturing and the sales departments to prepare a forecast, so that people are responsible for performing against their own predictions.

At Intel we try to match the two parallel flows with as much precision as possible. If there's no match, we end up with a customer order that we can't satisfy or with a finished product for which we have no customer. Either way we have problems. Obviously, if the match does come off, with a forecasted order becoming a real order,

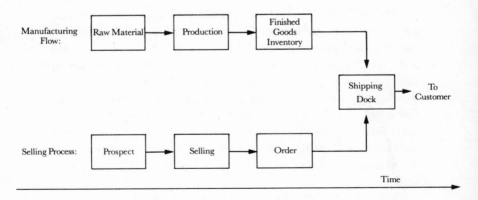

The order for the product and the product itself should arrive at the shipping dock at the same time.

the customer's requirements can be nicely satisfied with the factory's product delivery.

The ideal is rarely found in the real world. More often, customer orders don't develop in time or the customer changes his mind. As for the other flow, manufacturing could miss deadlines, or make mistakes, or encounter unforeseen problems. Because neither the sales flow nor the manufacturing flow is completely predictable, we should deliberately build a reasonable amount of *"slack"* into the system. And inventory is the most obvious place for it. Clearly, the more inventory we have, the more change we can cope with and still satisfy orders. But inventory costs money to build and keep, and therefore should be controlled carefully. Ideally, inventory should be kept at the *lowest-value stage,* as we've learned before, like raw eggs kept at the breakfast factory. Also, the lower the value, the more production flexibility we obtain for a given inventory cost.

It is a good idea to use stagger charts in both the manufacturing and sales forecasts. As noted, they will show the trend of change from one forecast to another, as well as the actual results. By repeatedly observing the variance of one forecast from another, you will continually pin down the causes of inaccuracy and improve your ability to forecast both orders and the availability of product.

Forecasting future work demands and then adjusting the output of an "administrative factory" represents a very important way in which its productivity can be increased. Though an old and honored way of operating "widget factories," the application of forecasting techniques is hardly common as a way to control administrative work. Such work has up to now been considered qualitatively different from work in a widget factory, and has also lacked objective performance standards needed to size or scale the work unit.

But if we have carefully chosen indicators that characterize an administrative unit and watch them closely, we are ready to apply the methods of factory control to administrative work. We can use de facto standards, inferred from the trend data, to forecast the number of people needed to accomplish various anticipated tasks. By rigorous application of the principles of forecasting, manpower can be reassigned from one area to another, and the headcount made to match the forecasted growth or decline in administrative activity. Without rigor, the staffing of administrative units would always be left at its highest level and, given Parkinson's famous law, people would find ways to let whatever they're doing fill the time available for its completion. There is no question that having standards and believing in them and staffing an administrative unit objectively using forecasted workloads will help you to maintain and enhance productivity.

Assuring Quality

As we have said, manufacturing's charter is to deliver product at a quality level acceptable to the customer at minimum cost. To assure that the quality of our product will in fact be acceptable, all production flows, whether they "make" breakfasts, college graduates, or software modules, must possess inspection points. To get acceptable quality at the lowest cost, it is vitally important to reject defective material at a stage where its accumulated value is at the lowest possible level. Thus, as noted, we are better off catching a bad raw egg than a cooked one, and screening out our college applicant before he visits Intel. In short, reject before investing further value.

In the language of production, the lowest-value-point inspection where we inspect raw material is called *incoming material inspection* or *receiving inspection*. If we again use a black box to represent our production process, inspections that occur at intervening points within it are called, logically enough, *in-process* inspections. Finally, the last possible point of inspection, when the product is ready to be shipped to the customer, is called *final inspection* or *outgoing quality inspection.* The three types are depicted below.

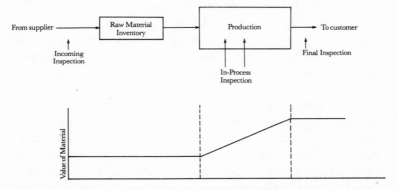

The key principle is to reject the defective "material" at its lowest-value stage.

When material is rejected at incoming inspection, a couple of choices present themselves. We can send it back to the vendor as unacceptable, or we can waive our specifications and use the substandard material anyway. The latter would result in a higher reject rate in our production process than if we had used thoroughly acceptable material, but that might be less expensive than shutting down the factory altogether until our vendor provides better material. Such decisions can only be made properly by a balanced group of managers, which typically consists of representatives from the quality assurance, manufacturing, and design engineering departments. This group can weigh all the consequences of rejecting or accepting substandard raw material.

While in most instances the decision to accept or reject defective material at a given inspection point is an economic one, one should *never* let substandard material

proceed when its defects could cause a complete failure
—a *reliability problem*—for our customer. Simply put, because we can never assess the consequences of an unreli-
able product, we can't make compromises when it comes
to reliability. Think of a component going into the making of a cardiac pacemaker. If some of the components
don't work upon receipt by the manufacturer, he can
replace them while the unit is still in the factory. This will
probably increase costs. But if the component fails later,
after the pacemaker has been implanted, the cost of the
failure is much more than a financial one.

Inspections, of course, cost money to perform and
further add to expense by interfering with the manufacturing flow and making it more complicated. Some material has to be recycled through steps already performed,
upsetting the smoothness with which the, rest of the material moves. Accordingly, one should approach the
need to inspect recognizing that a balance exists between
the desired result of the inspection, improved quality,
and minimum disturbance to the production process itself.

Let's consider a few techniques commonly used to
balance the two needs. There is a *gate-like* inspection and
a *monitoring* step. In the former, all material is held at the
"gate" until the inspection tests are completed. If the
material passes, it is moved on to the next stage in the
production process; if the material fails, it will be returned to an earlier stage, where it will be reworked or
scrapped. In the latter, a sample of the material is taken,
and if it fails, a notation is made from which a failure rate
is calculated. The bulk of the material is not held as the
sample is taken but continues to move through the
manufacturing process. The smoothness of the flow is
maintained, but if, for example, three successive samples
fail the monitoring test, we can stop the line. What is the
trade-off here? If we hold all the material, we add to
throughput time and slow down the manufacturing pro-

cess. A monitor produces no comparable slowdown but might let some bad material escape before we can act on the monitor's results and shut things down, which means that we might have to reject material later at a higher-value stage. Clearly, for the same money we can do a lot more monitoring than gate-type inspections; if we do the former, we may well contribute more to the overall quality of the product than if we choose less frequent gate-like inspections. The trade-off here is not obvious, and any choice has to be made with a specific case in mind. As a rule of thumb, we should lean toward monitoring when experience shows we are not likely to encounter big problems.

Another way to lower the cost of quality assurance is to use *variable inspections.* Because quality levels vary over time, it is only common sense to vary how often we inspect. For instance, if for weeks we don't find problems, it would seem logical to check less often. But if problems begin to develop, we can test ever more frequently until quality again returns to the previous high levels. The advantage here is still lower costs and even less interference with the production flow. Yet this approach is not used very often, even in widget manufacturing. Why not? Probably because we are creatures of habit and keep doing things the way we always have, whether it be from week to week or year to year.

Suitably thought through, intelligent inspection schemes can actually increase the efficiency and productivity of any manufacturing or administrative process. Let's take an example very different from the making of widgets or breakfasts.

I recently read a story in a news magazine that said that the American Embassy in London could not deal with a deluge of visa applications. Some one million Britons apply for visas each year, of which about 98 percent are approved. The embassy employs sixty people, who process as many as 6,000 applications a day. Most applications are received by mail, and at any time, from 60,000 to 80,000 British passports are in the embassy's hands. Meanwhile, lines of one hundred or more British and other nationals stand in front of the building, looking for an opportunity to walk their passports through. The embassy has tried a number of ways to handle matters more efficiently, including newspaper advertisements asking tourists to apply early and to expect a three-week turnaround. The embassy also installed boxes where applicants could drop off their passports and visa applications if they really needed same-day service. Even so, the lines at the embassy remained long.

In fact, the embassy's expediting schemes only made the problem worse, because nothing was done to address the basic issue: to speed the processing of visas overall. Time and money were spent to classify various kinds of applications slated for different processing times, but this only created more logistical overhead with no effect on output.

If our government wants British tourists to visit the United States, our government should not irritate these would-be visitors. And if the embassy can't get the money to increase its staff, a simple solution can be borrowed from basic production techniques. We need, in short, to replace their present scheme with a quality assurance test.

For that, the bureaucratic minds at the embassy would need to accept that a 100 percent check of the visa applicants is unnecessary. Some 98 percent of those applying are approved without any question. So if the embassy were to institute a sampling test of visas (a quality assurance test), and a thorough one at that, the logjam of applications could be broken without materially increasing the chance that the undesirable will enter our country. Moreover, the embassy could select the sample to be checked according to predetermined criteria. The visa processing could then work rather like the Internal Revenue Service. Through the checks and audits that the IRS performs, that government agency induces compliance among most taxpayers without having an agent look at every single return.

Later, when we examine managerial productivity, we'll see that when a manager digs deeply into a specific activity under his jurisdiction, he's applying the principle of variable inspection. If the manager examined everything his various subordinates did, he would be meddling, which for the most part would be a waste of his time. Even worse, his subordinates would become accustomed to not being responsible for their own work, knowing full well that their supervisor will check everything out closely. The principle of variable inspection applied to managerial work nicely skirts both problems, and, as we shall see, gives us an important tool for improving managerial productivity.

Productivity

The workings of our black box can furnish us with the simplest and most useful definition of productivity. The productivity of any function occurring within it is the output divided by the labor required to generate the output. Thus, one way to increase productivity is to do whatever we are now doing, but *faster*. This could be done by reorganizing the work area or just by working harder. Here we've not changed what work we do, we've just instituted ways to do it faster—getting more *activities per employee-hour* to go on inside the black box. Because the output of the black box is proportional to the activity that occurs within it, we will get more output per hour.

There is a second way to improve productivity. We can change the *nature* of the work performed: what we do, not how fast we do it. We want to increase the ratio of output to activity, thereby increasing output even if the activity per employee-hour remains the same. As the

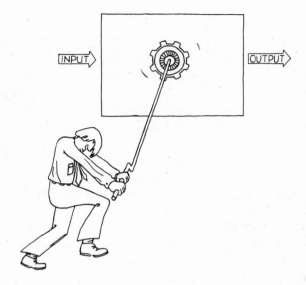

Productivity can be increased by performing the work activities at a higher rate . . .

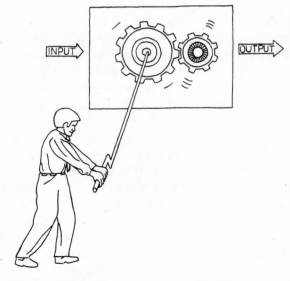

. . . or by increasing the **leverage** *of the activities.*

slogan has it, we want to "work smarter, not harder."

Here I'd like to introduce the concept of *leverage*, which is the output generated by a specific type of work activity. An activity with high leverage will generate a high level of output; an activity with low leverage, a low level of output. For example, a waiter able to boil two eggs and operate two toasters can deliver two breakfasts for almost the same amount of work as one. His output per activity, and therefore his leverage, is high. A waiter who can handle only one egg and one toaster at a time possesses lower output and leverage. The software engineer using a programming language rather like English, later to be translated by a compiler, can solve many problems per hour of programming. His output and leverage are high. A software engineer using a more cumbersome programming method of ones and zeros will require many more hours to solve the same number of problems. His output and leverage are low. Thus, a very important way to increase productivity is to arrange the work flow inside our black box so that it will be characterized by high output per activity, which is to say high-leverage activities.

Automation is certainly one way to improve the leverage of all types of work. Having machines to help them, human beings can create more output. But in both widget manufacturing and administrative work, something else can also increase the productivity of the black box. This is called *work simplification.* To get leverage this way, you first need to create a flow chart of the production process as it exists. Every single step must be shown on it; no step should be omitted in order to pretty things up on paper. Second, count the number of steps in the flow chart so that you know how many you started with. Third, set a rough target for reduction of the number of steps. In the first round of work simplification, our experience shows that you can reasonably expect a 30 to 50 percent reduction.

To implement the actual simplification, you must question *why* each step is performed. Typically, you will find that many steps exist in your work flow for no good reason. Often they are there by tradition or because formal procedure ordains it, and nothing practical requires their inclusion. Remember, the "visa factory" at our embassy in Britain didn't really have to process 100 percent of the applicants. So no matter what reason may be given for a step, you must critically question each and throw out those that common sense says you can do without. We found that in a wide range of administrative activities at Intel, substantial reduction—about 30 percent—could be achieved in the number of steps required to perform various tasks.

Of course, the principle of work simplification is hardly new in the widget manufacturing arts. In fact, this is one of the things industrial engineers have been doing for a hundred years. But the application of the principle to improve the productivity of the "soft professions"— the administrative, professional, and managerial workplace—is new and slow to take hold. The major problem to be overcome is defining what the output of such work is or should be. As we will see, in the work of the soft professions, it becomes very difficult to distinguish between output and activity. And as noted, stressing output is the key to improving productivity, while looking to increase activity can result in just the opposite.

Part Two

MANAGEMENT IS A TEAM GAME

3
Managerial
Leverage

What Is a Manager's Output?

I asked a group of middle managers just that question.
I got these responses:

    judgments and opinions
    direction
    allocation of resources
    mistakes detected
    personnel trained and subordinates developed
    courses taught
    products planned
    commitments negotiated

Do these things really constitute the output of a manager? I don't think so. They are instead *activities,* or de-
scriptions of what managers *do* as they try to create a final
result, or output. What, then, is a manager's output? At
Intel, if he is in charge of a wafer fabrication plant, his
output consists of completed, high-quality, fully processed silicon wafers. If he supervises a design group, his
output consists of completed designs that work correctly
and are ready to go into manufacturing. If a manager is
the principal of a high school, his output will be trained

and educated students who have either completed their schooling or are ready to move on to the next year of their studies. If a manager is a surgeon, his output is a fully recovered, healed patient. We can sum matters up with the proposition that:

$$\text{A manager's output} = \begin{array}{l} \text{The output of his organization} \\ + \\ \text{The output of the neighboring} \\ \text{organizations under his influence} \end{array}$$

Why? Because business and education and even surgery represent work done by *teams*.

A manager can do his "own" job, his individual work, and do it well, but that does not constitute his output. If the manager has a group of people reporting to him or a circle of people influenced by him, the manager's output must be measured by the output created by his subordinates and associates. If the manager is a knowledge specialist, a *know-how manager,* his potential for influencing "neighboring" organizations is enormous. The internal consultant who supplies needed insight to a group struggling with a problem will affect the work and the output of the entire group. Similarly, if a lawyer acquires a regulatory permit for a drug company, he will release the flow of the result of many years of research at that company to the public. Or a marketing analyst who reviews mountains of product, market, and competitive information, analyzes market research, and makes fact-finding visits can directly affect the output of many "neighboring" organizations. His interpretations of the data and his recommendations will perhaps guide the activities for the whole company. Thus, the definition of "manager" should be broadened: individual contributors who gather and disseminate know-how and information should also be seen as middle managers, because they exert great power within the organization.

But the key definition here is that the output of a manager is a result achieved by a group either under his supervision or under his influence. While the manager's own work is clearly very important, that in itself does not create output. His organization does. By analogy, a coach or a quarterback alone does not score touchdowns and win games. Entire teams with their participation and guidance and direction do. League standings are kept by team, not by individual. Business—and this means not just the business of commerce but the business of education, the business of government, the business of medicine—is a team activity. And, always, it takes a team to win.

It is important to understand that a manager will find himself engaging in an array of activities in order to affect output. As the middle managers I queried said, a manager must form opinions and make judgments, he must provide direction, he must allocate resources, he must detect mistakes, and so on. All these are necessary to achieve output. But output and activity are by no means the same thing.

Consider my own managerial role. As president of a company, I can affect output through my direct subordinates—group general managers and others like them—by performing supervisory activities. I can also influence groups not under my direct supervision by making observations and suggestions to those who manage them. Both types of activity will, I hope, contribute to my output as a manager by contributing to the output of the company as a whole. I was once asked by a middle manager at Intel how I could teach in-plant courses, visit manufacturing plants, concern myself with the problems of people several levels removed from me in the organization, and still have time to do my job. I asked him what he thought my job was. He thought for a moment, and then answered his own question, "I guess those things are your job too, aren't they?" They are absolutely my job—not my entire job, but part of it, because they help add to the output of Intel.

Let me give another example. Cindy, an engineer at Intel, supervises an engineering group in a wafer fabrication plant. She also spends some of her time as a member of an advisory body that establishes standard procedures by which all the plants throughout the company perform a certain technical process. In both roles, Cindy contributes to the output of the wafer fabrication plants. As a supervising engineer, she performs activities that increase the output of the plant in which she works; as a member of the advisory body, she provides specialized knowledge that will influence and increase the output of "neighboring organizations"—all the other Intel wafer fabrication plants.

Let's refer again to our black box. If the machinery within an organization can be compared to a series of gears, we can visualize how a middle manager affects output. In times of crisis, he provides power to the organization. When things aren't working as smoothly as they should, he applies a bit of oil. And, of course, he provides intelligence to the machine to direct its purpose.

"Daddy, What Do You Really Do?"

Most of us have had to struggle to answer that question. What we actually do is difficult to pin down and sum up. Much of it often seems so inconsequential that our position in the business hardly seems justified. Part of the problem here stems from the distinction between our activities, which is what we actually do, and our output, which is what we achieve. The latter seems important, significant, and worthwhile. The former often seems trivial, insignificant, and messy. But a surgeon whose output is a cured patient spends his time scrubbing and cutting and suturing, and this hardly sounds very respectable either.

To find out what we managers really do, let's take a look at one of my busier days, shown in the table below. Here I describe the activity in which I was engaged, explain it a bit, and categorize it into types we shall examine in the balance of the chapter.

A Day from My Life

Time and Activity	Explanation (Type of Activity)
8:00–8:30 Met with a manager who had submitted his resignation to leave for another company.	I listened to his reasons (*information-gathering*), felt he could be turned around and saved for Intel. Encouraged him to talk to certain other managers about a career change (*nudge*), and decided to pursue this matter with them myself (*decision-making*).
Incoming telephone call from a competitor.	Call was ostensibly about a meeting of an industry-wide society, but in reality he was feeling out how I saw business conditions. I did the same. (*Information-gathering.*)
8:30–9:00 Read mail from the previous afternoon.	I scribbled messages on about half of it, some of which were expressions of encouragement or disapproval, others exhortations to take certain types of action (*nudges*). One was the denial of a request to proceed

Time and Activity	Explanation (Type of Activity)
	with a particular small project *(decision-making)*. (Of course, *information-gathering* took place in all of these cases, too.)
9:00–12:00 Executive Staff Meeting (a regular weekly meeting of the company's senior management). Subjects covered at this particular one:	
—Review of the prior month's incoming order and shipment rates.	*(Information-gathering)*
—Discussion to set priorities for the upcoming annual planning process.	*(Decision-making)*
—Review of the status of a major marketing program (scheduled subject).	This came about through a prior decision that this program was faltering and required review. We found it was doing a little bit better than before *(information-gathering)*, but the presentation still elicited a lot of comments and suggestions *(nudges)* from various members of the audience.
—Review of a program to reduce the manufacturing cycle time of a particular product line (scheduled subject).	The presentation indicated that the program was in good shape. (It represented only *information-gathering;* no further action was stimulated.)

Time and Activity	Explanation (Type of Activity)
12:00–1:00 Lunch in the company cafeteria.	I happened to sit with members of our training organization, who complained about the difficulty they had in getting me and other senior managers to participate in training at our foreign locations *(information-gathering)*. This was news to me. I made a note to follow up with my own schedule, as well as with my staff, and to *nudge* them into doing a better job supporting the foreign training program.
1:00–2:00 Meeting regarding a specific product-quality problem.	The bulk of the meeting involved getting sufficient information on the status of the product and the corrective action that had been implemented *(information-gathering)*. The meeting ended in a *decision* made by the division manager, with my concurrence, to resume shipment of the product.
2:00–4:00 Lecture at our employee orientation program.	This is a program in which senior management gives all professional employees a presentation describing the objectives, history, management

Time and Activity	Explanation (Type of Activity)
	systems, etc., of the company and its major groups. I am the first lecturer in the series. This clearly represented *information-giving*, and I was a *role model* not only in communicating the importance we place on training, but also, by my handling of questions and comments, in representing, in living form, some of the values of the company. The nature of the questions, at the same time, gave me a feeling for the concerns and understanding level of a large number of employees to whom I would not otherwise have access. So this also represented *information-gathering*, characteristic of the "visit" type in its efficiency.
4:00–4:45 In the office, returning phone calls.	I disapproved granting a compensation increase to a particular employee, which I thought was way outside of the norm (clearly a *decision*). I decided to conduct a meeting with a group of people to decide what organization would move to a new site we were opening in another state. (This was a *decision* to hold a decision-making meeting.)
4:45–5:00 Met with my assistant.	Discussed a variety of re-

Time and Activity	Explanation (Type of Activity)
	quests for my time for a number of meetings in the upcoming week. Suggested alternatives where I *decided* not to attend.
5:00–6:15 Read the day's mail, including progress reports.	As with the morning's mail reading, this was *information-gathering*, interspersed with *nudging* and *decision-making* through my annotations and messages scribbled on much of it.

When you look at what happened, you won't see any obvious patterns. I dealt with things in seemingly random fashion. My wife's reaction to my day was that it looked very much like one of her own. She was right in noting a similarity. My day always ends when I'm tired and ready to go home, not when I'm done. I am never done. Like a housewife's, a manager's work is never done. There is always more to be done, more that should be done, always more than can be done.

A manager must keep many balls in the air at the same time and shift his energy and attention to activities that will most increase the output of his organization. In other words, he should move to the point where his *leverage* will be the greatest.

As you can see, much of my day is spent acquiring information. And as you can also see, I use many ways to get it. I read standard reports and memos but also get information ad hoc. I talk to people inside and outside the company, managers at other firms or financial analysts or members of the press. Customer complaints, both external and internal, are also a very important source of information. For example, the Intel training organization, which I serve as an instructor, is an internal customer of mine. To cut myself off from the casual complaints of people in that group would be a mistake because I would miss getting an evaluation of my performance as an internal "supplier." People also tell us things because they want us to do something for them; to advance their case, they will sometimes shower us with useful information. This is something we should remember, apart from whether we do as they ask.

I have to confess that the information most useful to me, and I suspect most useful to all managers, comes from quick, often casual verbal exchanges. This usually reaches a manager much faster than anything written down. And usually the more timely the information, the more valuable it is.

So why are written reports necessary at all? They obviously can't provide timely information. What they do is constitute an archive of data, help to validate ad hoc inputs, and catch, in safety-net fashion, anything you may have missed. But reports also have another totally different function. As they are formulated and written, the author is forced to be more precise than he might be verbally. Hence their value stems from the discipline and the thinking the writer is forced to impose upon himself as he identifies and deals with trouble spots in his presentation. Reports are more a *medium* of *self-discipline* than a way to communicate information. *Writing* the report is important; reading it often is not.

There are many parallels to this. As we will see later, the *preparation* of an annual plan is in itself the end, not the resulting bound volume. Similarly, our capital authorization *process* itself is important, not the authorization itself. To prepare and justify a capital spending request, people go through a lot of soul-searching analysis and juggling, and it is this mental exercise that is valuable.

The formal authorization is useful only because it enforces the discipline of the process.

To improve and maintain your capacity to get information, you have to understand the way it comes to you. There's a hierarchy involved. Verbal sources are the most valuable, but what they provide is also sketchy, incomplete, and sometimes inaccurate, like a newspaper headline that can give you only the general idea of a story. A headline can't give any of the details and might even give you a distorted idea of what the real story is. So you then read the newspaper article itself to find out who, what, where, why, and how. After this, you should have some reiteration and perspective, which can be compared to reading a news magazine or even a book. Each level in your information hierarchy is important, and you can rely on none alone. Though the most thorough information might come from the news magazine, you do not, of course, want to wait a full week after an event to find out about it. Your information sources should complement one another, and also be redundant because that gives you a way to verify what you've learned.

There is an especially efficient way to get information, much neglected by most managers. That is to visit a particular place in the company and observe what's going on there. Why should you do this? Think of what happens when somebody comes to see a manager in his office. A certain stop-and-start dynamics occurs when the visitor sits down, something socially dictated. While a two-minute kernel of information is exchanged, the meeting often takes a half hour. But if a manager walks through an area and sees a person with whom he has a two-minute concern, he can simply stop, cover it, and be on his way. Ditto for the subordinate when he initiates conversation. Accordingly, such visits are an extremely effective and efficient way to transact managerial business.

Then why are they underutilized? Because of the awkwardness that managers feel about walking through an area without a specific task in mind. At Intel we combat this problem by using programmed visits meant to accomplish formal tasks, but which also set the stage for ad hoc mini-transactions. For example, we ask our managers to participate in "Mr. Clean" inspections, in which they go to a part of the company that they normally wouldn't visit. The managers examine the housekeeping, the arrangement of things, the labs, and the safety equipment, and in so doing spend an hour or so browsing around and getting acquainted with things firsthand.

As can be seen from my schedule, a manager not only gathers information but is also a source of it. He must convey his knowledge to members of his own organization and to other groups he influences. Beyond relaying facts, a manager must also communicate his objectives, priorities, and preferences as they bear on the way certain tasks are approached. This is extremely important, because only if the manager imparts these will his subordinates know how to make decisions themselves that will be acceptable to the manager, their supervisor. Thus, transmitting objectives and preferred approaches constitutes a key to successful delegation. As we will see later, a shared corporate culture becomes indispensable to a business. Someone adhering to the values of a corporate culture—an intelligent corporate citizen—will behave in consistent fashion under similar conditions, which means that managers don't have to suffer the inefficiencies engendered by formal rules, procedures, and regulations that are sometimes used to get the same result.

The third major kind of managerial activity, of course, is decision-making. To be sure, once in a while we managers in fact *make* a decision. But for every time that happens, we *participate* in the making of many, many others, and we do that in a variety of ways. We provide factual inputs or just offer opinions, we debate the pros and cons of alternatives and thereby force a better decision to emerge, we review decisions made or about to be made by others, encourage or discourage them, ratify or veto them.

Just how decisions should be made, we'll talk about later. Meanwhile, let's say that decisions can be separated into two kinds. The forward-looking sort are made, for example, in the capital authorization process. Here we allocate the financial resources of the company among various future undertakings. The second type is made as we respond to a developing problem or a crisis, which can either be technical (a quality control problem, for example) or involve people (talking somebody out of quitting).

It's obvious that your decision-making depends finally on how well you comprehend the facts and issues facing your business. This is why information-gathering is so important in a manager's life. Other activities—conveying information, making decisions, and being a role model for your subordinates—are all governed by the *base of information* that you, the manager, have about the tasks, the issues, the needs, and the problems facing your organization. In short, information-gathering is the basis of all other managerial work, which is why I choose to spend so much of my day doing it.

You often do things at the office designed to influence events slightly, maybe making a phone call to an associate suggesting that a decision be made in a certain way, or sending a note or a memo that shows how you see a particular situation, or making a comment during an oral presentation. In such instances you may be advocating a preferred course of action, but you are not issuing an instruction or a command. Yet you're doing something stronger than merely conveying information. Let's call it "nudging" because through it you nudge an individual or a meeting in the direction you would like. This is an immensely important managerial activity in which we engage all the time, and it should be carefully distinguished from decision-making that results in firm, clear directives. In reality, for every unambiguous decision we make, we probably nudge things a dozen times.

Finally, something more subtle pervades the day of all managers. While we move about, doing what we regard as our jobs, we are *role models* for people in our organization—our subordinates, our peers, and even our supervisors. Much has been said and written about a manager's need to be a leader. The fact is, no single managerial activity can be said to constitute leadership, and nothing leads as well as example. By this I mean something straightforward. Values and behavioral norms are simply not transmitted easily by talk or memo, but are conveyed very effectively by doing and doing *visibly*.

All managers need to act so that they can be seen exerting influence, but they should do so in their own way. Some of us feel comfortable dealing with large groups and talking about our feelings and values openly in that fashion. Others prefer working one-on-one with people in a quieter, more intellectual environment. These and other styles of leadership will work, but only if we recognize and consciously stress the need for us to be role models for people in our organization.

Don't think for a moment that the way I've described leadership applies only to large operations. An insurance agent in a small office who continually talks with personal friends on the phone imparts a set of values about permissible conduct to everyone working for him. A lawyer who returns to his office after lunch a little drunk does the same. On the other hand, a supervisor in a company, large or small, who takes his work seriously exemplifies to his associates the most important managerial value of all.

A great deal of a manager's work has to do with allocating resources: manpower, money, and capital. But the single most important resource that we allocate from one day to the next is our own time. In principle more money, more manpower, or more capital can always be made available, but our own time is the one absolutely finite resource we each have. Its allocation and use therefore deserve considerable attention. How you handle x your own time is, in my view, the single most important aspect of being a role model and leader.

As you can see, in a typical day of mine one can count some twenty-five separate activities in which I participated, mostly information-gathering and -giving, but also decision-making and nudging. You can also see that some two thirds of my time was spent in a meeting of one kind or another. Before you are horrified by how much time I spend in meetings, answer a question: which of the activities—information-gathering, information-giving, decision-making, nudging, and being a role model— could I have performed outside a meeting? The answer is practically none. Meetings provide an occasion for managerial activities. Getting together with others is not, ✓ of course, an activity—it is a *medium*. You as a manager can do your work in a meeting, in a memo, or through a loudspeaker for that matter. But you must choose the most effective medium for what you want to accomplish, and that is the one that gives you the greatest leverage. More about meetings later.

Leverage of Managerial Activity

We've established that the output of a manager is the output of the various organizations under his control and his influence. What can a manager do to increase his output? To find out, let's look at the concept of *leverage*. Leverage is the measure of the output generated by any given managerial activity. Accordingly, managerial output can be linked to managerial activity by the equation:

$$\text{Managerial Output} = \text{Output of organization}$$
$$= L_1 \times A_1 + L_2 \times A_2 + \ldots$$

This equation says that for every activity a manager performs—A_1, A_2, and so on—the output of the organization should increase by some degree. The extent to which that output is thereby increased is determined by the leverage of that activity—L_1, L_2, and so on. A manager's output is thus the sum of the result of individual activities having varying degrees of leverage. Clearly the key to high output means being sensitive to the *leverage* of what you do during the day.

Managerial productivity—that is, the output of a manager per unit of time worked—can be increased in three ways:

1. Increasing the rate with which a manager performs his activities, speeding up his work.
2. Increasing the leverage associated with the various managerial activities.
3. Shifting the mix of a manager's activities from those with lower to those with higher leverage.

Let us consider first the leverage of various types of managerial work.

HIGH-LEVERAGE ACTIVITIES

These can be achieved in three basic ways:

- When many people are affected by one manager.
- When a person's activity or behavior over a long period of time is affected by a manager's brief, well-focused set of words or actions.

- When a large group's work is affected by an individual supplying a unique, key piece of knowledge or information.

The first is the most obvious example. Consider Robin, an Intel finance manager, responsible for setting up the annual financial planning process for the company. When Robin defines in advance exactly what information needs to be gathered and presented at each stage of the planning process and lays out who is responsible for what, she directly affects the subsequent work of perhaps two hundred people who participate in the planning process. By spending a certain amount of time *in* advance of the planning activities, Robin will help to eliminate confusion and ambiguity for a large population of managers over an extended period of time. Consequently, her work contributes to the productivity of the entire organization and clearly has great leverage, leverage that depends, however, on *when* it is performed. Work done in advance of the planning meeting obviously has great leverage. If Robin has to scramble later to help a manager define guidelines and milestones, her work will clearly have much less leverage.

Another example of leverage that depends on timely action is what you do when you learn that a valued subordinate has decided to quit. In such a case, you must direct yourself to the situation immediately if you want to change the person's mind. If you put it off, all your chances are lost. Thus to maximize the leverage of his activities, a manager must keep *timeliness,* which is often critical, firmly in mind.

Leverage can also be negative. Some managerial activities can *reduce* the output of an organization. I mean something very simple. Suppose I am a key participant at a meeting and I arrive unprepared. Not only do I waste the time of the people attending the meeting because of my lack of preparation—a direct cost of my carelessness —but I deprive the other participants of the opportunity to use that time to do something else.

Each time a manager imparts his knowledge, skills, or values to a group, his leverage is high, as members of the group will carry what they learn to many others. But again, leverage can be positive or negative. An example of leverage that I hope is high and positive is my talk in the orientation course. During the two hours I have, I try to impart a great deal of information about Intel—its history, its objectives, its values, its style—to a group of two hundred new employees. Besides what I say specifically, my approach toward answering questions and my conduct in general communicate our way of doing things to these employees when they are most impressionable.

Here is another example of this kind of leverage. To train a group of salesmen, Barbara, an Intel marketing engineer, sets out to teach them what the organization's products are. If she does her job well, the salespeople will be better equipped to sell the line. If she does it poorly, great and obvious damage is done.

A final, less formal, example here: Cindy, as you recall, is a member of a technical coordinating body in which she tries to disseminate her understanding of a specific technology to all of the company's manufacturing groups. In effect, she uses the coordinating body as an informal training vehicle to effect high leverage on her counterparts in neighboring Intel organizations.

A manager can also exert high leverage by engaging in an activity that takes him only a *short* time, but that affects another person's performance over a *long* time. A performance review represents a good example of this. With the few hours' work that a manager spends preparing and delivering the review, he can affect the work of its recipient enormously. Here too a manager can exert either positive or negative leverage. A subordinate can be motivated and even redirected in his efforts, or the review can discourage and demoralize him for who knows how long.

Another seemingly trivial piece of work—creating a tickler file—can improve daily work significantly for a long time. Setting up the simple mechanical aid is a one-time activity, yet it is likely to improve the productivity of the manager who uses it indefinitely. Thus the leverage here is very, very high.

Examples of high negative leverage abound. After going through the annual planning process, an Intel manager saw that, in spite of successful cost reduction efforts in the prior year, his division was still not going to make any money in the coming year. The manager became depressed. Though he didn't realize it, he almost immediately began to affect people around him and soon depression spread throughout his organization. He snapped out of it only when someone on his staff finally told him what he was doing to the people under him. Another example is waffling, when a manager puts off a decision that will affect the work of other people. In effect, the lack of a decision is the same as a negative decision; no green light is a red light, and work can stop for a whole organization.

Both the depressed and the waffling manager can have virtually unlimited negative leverage. If people are badly affected by a poor sales training effort, the situation can be handled by retraining the group. But the negative leverage produced by depression and waffling is very hard to counter because their impact on an organization is both so pervasive and so elusive.

Managerial meddling is also an example of negative leverage. This occurs when a supervisor uses his superior knowledge and experience of a subordinate's responsibilities to assume command of a situation rather than letting the subordinate work things through himself. For example, if a senior manager sees an indicator showing an undesirable trend and dictates to the person responsible a detailed set of actions to be taken, that is managerial meddling. In general, meddling stems from a supervisor exploiting too much superior work knowledge (real or imagined). The negative leverage produced comes from the fact that after being exposed to many such instances, the subordinate will begin to take a much more restricted view of what is expected of him, showing less initiative in solving his own problems and referring them instead to his supervisor. Because the output of the organization will consequently be reduced in the long run, meddling is clearly an activity having negative managerial leverage.

The third kind of managerial activity with high leverage is exercised by a person with *unique skills* and *knowledge*. One such person is an Intel marketing engineer responsible for setting prices for the product line. Hundreds of salespeople in the field can be negatively affected if prices are set too high: no matter how hard they may try, they won't be able to get any business. Of course, if the prices were set too low, we would be giving money away.

Take another example. An Intel development engineer who has uniquely detailed knowledge of a particular manufacturing process effectively controls how it is used. Since the process will eventually provide the foundation for the work of many product designers all over the company, the leverage the development engineer exerts is enormous. The same is true for a geologist in an oil company or an actuary in an insurance firm. All are specialists whose work is important for the work of their organization at large. The person who comprehends the critical facts or has the critical insights—the "knowledge specialist" or the "know-how manager"—has tremendous authority and influence on the work of others, and therefore very high leverage.

The *art* of management lies in the capacity to select from the many activities of seemingly comparable significance the one or two or three that provide leverage well beyond the others and concentrate on them. For me, paying close attention to customer complaints consti- ✓ tutes a high-leverage activity. Aside from making a customer happy, the pursuit tends to produce important insights into the workings of my own operation. Such complaints may be numerous, and though all of them need to be followed up by someone, they don't all require or wouldn't all benefit from my personal attention. Which one out of ten or twenty complaints to dig into, analyze, and follow up is where art comes into the work of a manager. The basis of that art is an intuition that behind this complaint and not the other lurk many deeper problems.

DELEGATION AS LEVERAGE

Because managerial time has a hierarchy of values, delegation is an essential aspect of management. The "delegator" and "delegatee" must share a common information base and a common set of operational ideas or notions on how to go about solving problems, a requirement that is frequently not met. Unless both parties share the relevant common base, the delegatee can become an effective proxy only with specific instructions. As in meddling, where specific activities are prescribed in detail, this produces low managerial leverage.

Picture this. I am your supervisor, and I walk over to you with pencil in hand and tell you to take it. You reach for the pencil, but I won't let go. So I say, "What is wrong with you? Why can't I delegate the pencil to you?" We all have some things that we don't really *want* to delegate simply because we like doing them and would rather not let go. For your managerial effectiveness, this is not too bad so long as it is based on a *conscious* decision that you will hold on to certain tasks that you enjoy performing, even though you could, if you chose, delegate them. But be sure to know exactly what you're doing, and avoid the charade of insincere delegation, which can produce immense negative managerial leverage.

Given a choice, should you delegate activities that are familiar to you or those that aren't? Before answering, consider the following principle: delegation without follow-through is *abdication*. You can never wash your hands of a task. Even after you delegate it, you are still responsible for its accomplishment, and monitoring the delegated task is the only practical way for you to ensure a result. Monitoring is not meddling, but means checking to make sure an activity is proceeding in line with expectations. Because it is easier to monitor something with which you are familiar, if you have a choice ∨ you should delegate those activities you know best. But recall the pencil experiment and understand before the fact that this will very likely go against your emotional grain.

Please turn back to the table of my day's activities on pages 43–47. During the executive staff meeting we heard two follow-up presentations, one on the status of an extremely important marketing program and the other on the progress of a program aimed at reducing manufacturing throughput times. Both reviews are examples of monitoring. Earlier, we had assigned each to a middle manager and made sure these managers and the senior staff agreed about what the programs were to be. The middle managers then went about their business expecting to report back to the executive staff, the body that delegated the programs to them.

Monitoring the results of delegation resembles the monitoring used in quality assurance. We should apply quality assurance principles and monitor at the lowest-added-value stage of the process. For example, review *rough drafts* of reports that you have delegated; don't wait until your subordinates have spent time polishing them into final form before you find out that you have a basic problem with the contents. A second principle applies to the frequency with which you check your subordinates' work. A variable approach should be employed, using different sampling schemes with various subordinates; you should increase or decrease your frequency depending on whether your subordinate is performing a newly delegated task or one that he has experience handling. How often you monitor should not be based on what you believe your subordinate can do *in general,* but on his experience with a specific task and his prior performance with it—his task-relevant maturity, something I'll talk about in detail later. As the subordinate's work improves over time, you should respond with a corresponding reduction in the intensity of the monitoring.

To use quality assurance principles effectively, the manager should only go into details randomly, just enough to try to ensure that the subordinate is moving ahead satisfactorily. To check into *all* the details of a delegated task would be like quality assurance testing 100 percent of what manufacturing turned out.

Making certain *types* of decisions is something managers frequently delegate to subordinates. How is this best done? By monitoring their decision-making *process.* How do you do that? Let's examine what Intel goes through to approve a capital equipment purchase. We ask a subordinate to think through the entire matter carefully before presenting a request for approval. And to monitor how good his thinking is, we ask him quite specific questions about his request during a review meeting. If he answers them convincingly, we'll approve what he wants. This technique allows us to find out how good the thinking is without having to go through it ourselves.

Increasing Managerial Activity Rate: Speeding Up the Line

Of course, the most obvious way to increase managerial output is to increase the *rate*, or speed, of performing work. The relationship here is:

$$\frac{\text{Managerial Output}}{\text{Time}} = \text{L} \times \frac{\text{Activity Performed}}{\text{Time}}$$

where L is the leverage of the activity.

The most common approach to increasing a manager's productivity—his output over time—has been time-management techniques, which try to reduce the denominator on both sides of this equation. Any number of consultants will tell a manager that the way to higher productivity is to handle a piece of paper only once, to hold only stand-up meetings (which will presumably be short), and to turn his desk so that he presents his back to the door.

These time-management suggestions can be improved upon, I think, by applying our production principles. First, we must identify our *limiting step:* what is the "egg" in our work? In a manager's life some things really have to happen on a schedule that is absolute. For me, an example is the class I teach. I know when it is going to meet, and I know I must prepare for it. There is no "give" in the time here, because over two hundred students will be expecting me. Accordingly, I have to create offsets and schedule my other work around this limiting step. In short, if we determine what is immovable and manipulate the more yielding activities around it, we can work more efficiently.

A second production principle we can apply to managerial work is *batching* similar tasks. Any manufacturing operation requires a certain amount of set-up time. So for managerial work to proceed efficiently, we should use the same set-up effort to apply across a group of similar activities. Think about our continuous egg-boiler, which was installed to produce fine-quality, identical, three-minute eggs. Should we now decide to serve our customers four-minute eggs, we would have to slow down the conveyor belt moving them through the hot water. The adjustment takes time: not only do we adjust nuts and bolts on the machine, we also have to inspect the quality of the four-minute eggs by sampling a few of them.

Set-up time has many parallels in managerial work. For example, once we have prepared a set of illustrations for a training class, we will obviously increase our productivity if we can use the same set over and over again with other classes or groups. Similarly, if a manager has a number of reports to read or a number of performance reviews to approve, he should set aside a block of time and do a batch of them together, one after the other, to maximize the use of the *mental* set-up time needed for the task.

What makes running a factory different from running a job shop? The latter is prepared to service any customer who drops in; the owner handles the job required and moves on to the next one. A factory, on the other hand, is usually run by *forecast* and not by individual order. From my experience a large portion of managerial work *can be* forecasted. Accordingly, forecasting those things you can and setting yourself up to do them is only common sense and an important way to minimize the feeling and the reality of fragmentation experienced in managerial work. Forecasting and planning your time √ around key events are literally like running an efficient factory.

What is the *medium* of a manager's forecast? It is something very simple: his *calendar*. Most people use their calendars as a repository of "orders" that come in. Someone throws an order to a manager for his time, and it automatically shows up on his calendar. This is mind-

less passivity. To gain better control of his time, the
✓ manager should use his calendar as a "production" planning tool, taking a firm initiative to schedule work that
is not time-critical between those "limiting steps" in the
day.

Another production principle can be applied here.
Because manufacturing people trust their indicators,
they won't allow material to begin its journey through
the factory if they think it is already operating at capacity. If they did, material might go halfway through and
back up behind a bottleneck. Instead, factory managers
✓ say "no" at the outset and keep the start level from
overloading the system. Other kinds of managers find
this hard to apply because their indicators of capacity
are not as well established or not as believable. How
much time do you need to read your mail, to write your
reports, to meet with a colleague? You may not know
precisely, but you surely have a feel for the time required. And you should exploit that sense to schedule
your work.

To use your calendar as a production-planning tool,
you must accept responsibility for two things:

1. You should move toward the *active* use of your calendar, taking the initiative to fill the holes between
the time-critical events with non-time-critical
though necessary activities.

✓ 2. You should say "no" at the outset to work beyond
your capacity to handle.

It is important to say "no" earlier rather than later
because we've learned that to wait until something
reaches a higher value stage and then abort due to lack
of capacity means losing more money and time. You can
obviously say "no" either explicitly or implicitly, because
by not delivering you end up saying what amounts to
"no." Remember too that your time is your one finite

resource, and when you say "yes" to one thing you are ∨ inevitably saying "no" to another.

The next production principle you can apply is to allow *slack*—a bit of looseness in your scheduling. High- ∨ way planners, for example, know that a freeway can handle an optimum number of vehicles. Having fewer cars means that the road is not being used at capacity. But at that optimum point, if just a few more cars are allowed to enter the traffic flow, everything comes to a crunching halt. With the new metering devices that control access during the rush hour, planners can get a fix on the right number. The same thing can be done for managerial work. There is an optimum degree of loading, with enough slack built in so that one unanticipated phone call will not ruin your schedule for the rest of the day. You need some slack.

Another production principle is very nearly the opposite. A manager should carry a raw material *inventory* in terms of projects. This is not to be confused with his work-in-process inventory, because that, like eggs in a continuous boiler, tends to spoil or become obsolete over time. Instead this inventory should consist of things you need to do but don't need to finish right away— discretionary projects, the kind the manager can work on to increase his group's productivity over the long term. Without such an inventory of projects, a manager will most probably use his free time *meddling* in his subordinates' work.

A final principle. Most production practices follow well-established procedures and, rather than reinventing the wheel repeatedly, use a specific method that has been shown to work before. But managers tend to be inconsistent and bring a welter of approaches to the same task. We should work to change that. As we become more consistent, we should also remember that the value of an administrative procedure is contained not in formal statements but in the real thinking that led to its establishment. This means that even as we try to standardize what we do, we should continue to think critically about what we do and the approaches we use.

Built-In Leverage: How Many Subordinates Should You Have . . .

An important component of managerial leverage is the number of subordinates a manager has. If he does not have enough, his leverage is obviously reduced. If he has too many, he gets bogged down—with the same result. As a rule of thumb, a manager whose work is largely supervisory should have six to eight subordinates; three or four are too few and ten are too many. This range comes from a guideline that a manager should allocate about a half day per week to each of his subordinates. (Two days a week per subordinate would probably lead to meddling; an hour a week does not provide enough opportunity for monitoring.)

The six to eight rule is right for the classically hierarchical manager whose primary work is the supervision of others. What about a know-how manager, the middle manager who mainly supplies expertise and information? Even if he works without a single subordinate, servicing a number of varied "customers" as an internal consultant can in itself be a full-time job. In fact, anyone who spends about a half day per week as a member of a planning, advisory, or coordinating group has the equivalent of a subordinate. So as a rule of thumb, if a manager is both a hierarchical supervisor and a supplier of know-how, he should try to have a total of six to eight subordinates or their equivalent.

Sometimes a business is organized in a way that makes the ideal fan-out of six to eight subordinates hard to reach. A manufacturing plant, for example, may have an engineering section and a production section, in which

case the plant manager would only have two people reporting directly to him. The manager might then choose
to "act" as one of the two subordinates, choosing to be
his own engineering manager, for instance. If he does
that, the manufacturing manager will still report to him,
and he will have added the people who would ordinarily
report to the head of engineering. So the plant manager
will actually have six direct reports: five engineers and
the manufacturing manager. The arrangement, shown
below, does not have the engineers *appearing to be* at the
same organizational level as the manufacturing manager
—something he would surely take exception to.

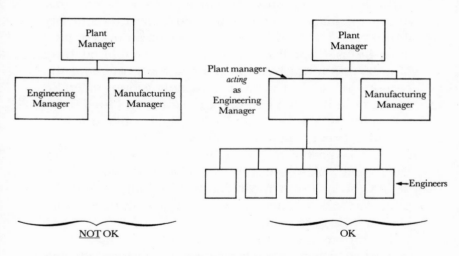

NOT OK   OK

*This arrangement will avoid forcing the plant manager either into
on-the-job retirement or into meddling.*

Interruptions—The Plague of Managerial Work

The next important production concept we can apply to
managerial work is to strive toward *regularity*. We could
obviously run our breakfast factory more efficiently if
customers arrived in a steady and predictable stream

rather than dropping in by ones and twos. Though we can't control our customers' habits, we should try to smooth out our workload as much as possible. As noted, we should try to make our managerial work take on the characteristics of a factory, not a job shop. Accordingly, we should do everything we can to prevent little stops and starts in our day as well as interruptions brought on by big emergencies. Even though some of the latter are unavoidable, we should always be looking for sources of future high-priority trouble by cutting windows into the black box of our organization. Recognizing you've got a time bomb on your hands means you can address a problem *when you want to,* not after the bomb has gone off.

But because you must coordinate your work with that of other managers, you can only move toward regularity if others do too. In other words, the same blocks of time must be used for like activities. For example, at Intel Monday mornings have been set aside throughout the corporation as the time when planning groups meet. So anybody who belongs to one can count on Monday for that purpose and be free of scheduling conflicts.

About twenty middle managers at Intel were once asked to be part of an experiment. After pairing up, they tried some role-playing in which one manager was to define the problem most limiting his output and the other was to be a consultant who would analyze the problem and propose solutions.

The most common problem cited was *uncontrolled interruptions,* which in remarkably uniform fashion affected both supervisory and know-how managers. Everyone felt that the interruptions got in the way of his "own" work. Interruptions had a common source, most frequently coming from subordinates and from people outside the managers' immediate organization but whose work the managers influenced. For those in manufacturing, the interruptions most often came from production operators, and for marketing people, from outside customers: in short, from the consumers of the middle managers' authority and information.

The most frequently proposed solutions were not very practical. The idea mentioned most often was to create blocks of time for individual work by hiding physically. But this is a less than happy answer, because the interrupters obviously have legitimate problems, and if the manager responded by hiding, these would pile up. One "solution" was a suggestion that customers not call marketing managers at certain hours. No good.

There are better ways. Let's apply a production concept. Manufacturers turn out *standard products.* By analogy, if you can pin down what kind of interruptions you're getting, you can prepare standard responses for those that pop up most often. Customers don't come up with totally new questions and problems day in and day out, and because the same ones tend to surface repeatedly, a manager can reduce time spent handling interruptions using standard responses. Having them available also means that a manager can delegate much of the job to less experienced personnel.

Also, if you use the production principle of *batching*— that is, handling a group of similar chores at one time— many interruptions that come from your subordinates can be accumulated and handled not randomly, but at staff and at one-on-one meetings, the subject of the next chapter. If such meetings are held regularly, people can't protest too much if they're asked to batch questions and problems for *scheduled* times, instead of interrupting you whenever they want.

The use of indicators, especially the bank of indicators kept over time, can also reduce the time a manager spends dealing with interruptions. How fast he can answer a question depends on how fast he can put his finger on the information he needs for a response. By maintaining an archive of information, a manager doesn't have to do ad hoc research every time the phone rings.

If the people who interrupt you knew how much they were disturbing you, they would probably police themselves more closely and cut down on the number of times they felt they had to talk to you right away. In any case, a manager should try to force his frequent interrupters to make an *active* decision about whether an issue can wait. So, instead of going into hiding, a manager can hang a sign on his door that says, "I am doing individual work. Please don't interrupt me unless it really can't wait until 2:00." Then hold an open office hour, and be completely receptive to anybody who wants to see you. The key is this: understand that interrupters have legitimate problems that need to be handled. That's why they're bringing them to you. But you can channel the time needed to deal with them into organized, scheduled form by providing an *alternative* to interruption—a scheduled meeting or an office hour.

The point is to impose a *pattern* on the way a manager copes with problems. To make something regular that was once irregular is a fundamental production principle, and that's how you should try to handle the interruptions that plague you.

4

Meetings— The Medium of Managerial Work

Meetings have a bad name. One school of management thought considers them the curse of the manager's existence. Someone who did a study found that managers spend up to 50 percent of their time in meetings, and implied that this was time wasted. Peter Drucker once said that spending more than 25 percent of his time in meetings is a sign of a manager's malorganization, and William H. Whyte, Jr., in his book *The Organization Man*, described meetings as "non-contributory labor" that managers must endure.

But there is another way to regard meetings. Earlier we said that a big part of a middle manager's work is to supply information and know-how, and to impart a sense of the preferred method of handling things to the groups under his control and influence. A manager also makes and helps to make decisions. Both kinds of basic managerial tasks can only occur during face-to-face encounters, and therefore only during meetings. Thus I will assert again that a meeting is nothing less than the *medium* through which managerial work is performed. That means we should not be fighting their very existence, but rather using the time spent in them as efficiently as possible.

The two basic managerial roles produce two basic kinds of meetings. In the first kind of meeting, called a *process-oriented* meeting, knowledge is shared and *information* is exchanged. Such meetings take place on a regularly scheduled basis. The purpose of the second kind of meeting is to solve a specific problem. Meetings of this sort, called *mission-oriented,* frequently produce a *decision.* They are ad hoc affairs, not scheduled long in advance, because they usually can't be.

Process-Oriented Meetings

To make the most of this kind of meeting, we should aim to infuse it with regularity. In other words, the people attending should know how the meeting is run, what kinds of substantive matters are discussed, and what is to be accomplished. It should be designed to allow a manager to "batch" transactions, to use the same "production" set-up time and effort to take care of many similar managerial tasks. Moreover, given the regularity, you and the others attending can begin to forecast the time required for the kinds of work to be done. Hence, a "production control" system, as recorded on various calendars, can take shape, which means that a scheduled meeting will have minimum impact on other things people are doing.

At Intel we use three kinds of process-oriented meetings: the one-on-one, the staff meeting, and the operation review.

ONE-ON-ONES

At Intel, a one-on-one is a meeting between a supervisor and a subordinate, and it is the principal way their business relationship is maintained. Its main purpose is mutual teaching and exchange of information. By talking about specific problems and situations, the supervisor teaches the subordinate his skills and know-how, and suggests ways to approach things. At the same time, the subordinate provides the supervisor with detailed information about what he is doing and what he is concerned about. From what I can tell, regularly scheduled one-on-ones are highly unusual outside of Intel. When I ask a manager from another company about the practice, I usually get an "Oh no, I don't need scheduled meetings with my supervisor [or subordinate]; I see him several times a day . . ." But there is an enormous difference between a casual encounter by a supervisor and a subordinate, or even a meeting (mission-oriented) to resolve a specific problem, and a one-on-one.

When Intel was a young company, I realized that even though I was expected to supervise both engineering and manufacturing, I knew very little about the company's first product line, memory devices. I also didn't know much about manufacturing techniques, my background having been entirely in semiconductor device research. So two of my associates, both of whom reported to me, agreed to give me private lessons on memory design and manufacturing. These took place by appointment, and involved a teacher/subordinate preparing for each; during the session the pupil/supervisor busily took notes, trying to learn. As Intel grew, the initial tone and spirit of such one-on-ones endured and grew.

Who should have a one-on-one? In some situations a supervisor should perhaps meet with all those who work under him, from professionals to production operators. But here I want to talk about one-on-ones between a supervisor and each of the professionals who report to him directly.

How often should you have one-on-ones? Or put another way, how do you decide how often somebody needs such a meeting? The answer is the *job-* or *task-relevant maturity* of each of your subordinates. In other words, how much experience does a given subordinate have with the specific task at hand? This is not the same as the experience he has in general or how old he is. As we will see later, the most effective management style in a specific instance varies from very close to very loose supervision as a subordinate's task maturity increases. Accordingly, you should have one-on-ones frequently (for example, once a week) with a subordinate who is inexperienced in a specific situation and less frequently (perhaps once every few weeks) with an experienced veteran.

Another consideration here is how quickly things change in a job area. In marketing, for example, the pace may be so rapid that a supervisor needs to have frequent one-on-ones to keep current on what's happening. But in a research environment, life may be quieter, and for a given level of task-relevant maturity, less frequent meetings may suffice.

How long should a one-on-one meeting last? There really is no answer to this, but the subordinate must feel that there is enough time to broach and get into thorny issues. Look at it this way. If you had a big problem that you wanted to kick around with your supervisor—the person whose professional interest in the matter is second only to yours—would you want to bring it up in a meeting scheduled to last only fifteen minutes? You would not. I feel that a one-on-one should last an hour at a minimum. Anything less, in my experience, tends to make the subordinate confine himself to simple things that can be handled quickly.

Where should a one-on-one take place? In the supervisor's office, in the subordinate's office, or somewhere else? I think you should have the meeting in or near the subordinate's work area if possible. A supervisor can learn a lot simply by going to his subordinate's office. Is he organized or not? Does he repeatedly have to spend time looking for a document he wants? Does he get interrupted all the time? Never? And in general, how does the subordinate approach his work?

A key point about a one-on-one: It should be regarded as the *subordinate's* meeting, with its agenda and tone set by him. There's good reason for this. Somebody needs to prepare for the meeting. The supervisor with eight subordinates would have to prepare eight times; the subordinate only once. So the latter should be asked to prepare an outline, which is very important because it forces him to think through in advance all of the issues and points he plans to raise. Moreover, with an outline, the supervisor knows at the outset what is to be covered and can therefore help to set the pace of the meeting according to the "meatiness" of the items on the agenda. An outline also provides a framework for supporting information, which the subordinate should prepare in advance. The subordinate should then walk the supervisor through all the material.

What should be covered in a one-on-one? We can start with performance figures, indicators used by the subordinate, such as incoming order rates, production output, or project status. Emphasis should be on indicators that signal trouble. The meeting should also cover anything important that has happened since the last meeting: current hiring problems, people problems in general, organizational problems and future plans, and—very, very important—*potential* problems. Even when a problem isn't tangible, even if it's only an intuition that something's wrong, a subordinate owes it to his supervisor to tell him, because it triggers a look into the organizational black box. The most important criterion governing matters to be talked about is that they be issues that preoccupy and nag the subordinate. These are often obscure and take time to surface, consider, and resolve.

What is the role of the supervisor in a one-on-one? He should facilitate the subordinate's expression of what's going on and what's bothering him. The supervisor is there to learn and to coach. Peter Drucker sums up the supervisor's job here very nicely: "The good time users among managers do not talk to their subordinates about their problems but they know how to make the subordinates talk about theirs."

How is this done? By applying Grove's Principle of ✓ Didactic Management, *"Ask one more question!"* When the supervisor thinks the subordinate has said all he wants to about a subject, he should ask another question. He should try to keep the flow of thoughts coming by prompting the subordinate with queries until *both* feel satisfied that they have gotten to the bottom of a problem.

I'd like to suggest some mechanical hints for effective one-on-one meetings. First, both the supervisor and subordinate should have a copy of the outline and both should take notes on it, which serves a number of purposes. I take notes in just about all circumstances, and most often end up never looking at them again. I do it to keep my mind from drifting and also to help me digest the information I hear and see. Since I take notes in outline form, I am forced to categorize the information logically, which helps me to absorb it. Equally important is what "writing it down" symbolizes. Many issues in a one-on-one lead to action required on the part of the subordinate. When he takes a note immediately following the supervisor's suggestion, the act implies a com-✓ mitment, like a handshake, that something will be done. The supervisor, also having taken notes, can then follow up at the next one-on-one.

A real time-saver is using a "hold" file where both the supervisor and subordinate accumulate important but not altogether urgent issues for discussion at the next meeting. This kind of file applies the production principle of batching and saves time for both involved by minimizing the need for ad hoc contact—like phone calls, drop-in visits, and so on—which constitute the interruptions we considered earlier.

The supervisor should also encourage the discussion of heart-to-heart issues during one-on-ones, because this is the perfect forum for getting at subtle and deep work-related problems affecting his subordinate. Is he satisfied with his own performance? Does some frustration or obstacle gnaw at him? Does he have doubts about where he is going? But the supervisor should be wary of the "zinger," which is a heart-to-heart issue brought up at an awkward time. More often than not, these come near the end of a meeting. If you let that happen, the subordinate might tell you something like he's unhappy and has been looking outside for a job and give you only five minutes to deal with it.

Long-distance telephone one-on-ones have become necessary because many organizations are now spread out geographically. But these can work well enough with proper preparation and attention: the supervisor must have the outline before the meeting begins, both parties should take notes, and so on. Because you can't see the other participant in the meeting, note-taking can't work in the same way as in a face-to-face meeting. Exchanging notes after the meeting is a way to make sure each knows what the other committed himself to do.

One-on-ones should be scheduled on a rolling basis—setting up the next one as the meeting taking place ends. Other commitments can thereby be taken into account and cancellations avoided. If the supervisor uses a set schedule for a one-on-one, such as every second Wednesday morning, and if the subordinate's vacation happens to fall on that date, the meeting is not going to occur. By scheduling on a rolling basis, this can be easily avoided.

What is the leverage of the one-on-one? Let's say you have a one-on-one with your subordinate every two weeks, and it lasts one and a half hours. Ninety minutes of your time can enhance the quality of your subordinate's work for two weeks, or for some eighty-plus hours, and also upgrade your understanding of what he's doing. Clearly, one-on-ones can exert enormous leverage. This happens through the development of a common base of information and similar ways of doing and handling things between the supervisor and the subordinate. And this, as noted, is the only way in which efficient and effective delegation can take place.

At the same time, the subordinate teaches the supervisor, and what is learned is absolutely essential if the supervisor is to make good decisions. During a recent one-on-one meeting, my subordinate, who is responsible for Intel's sales organization, reviewed trend indicators of incoming orders. While I was vaguely familiar with them, he laid out a lot of specific information and convinced me that our business had stopped growing. Even though the summer is typically slow, he proved to me that what was going on was not just seasonal. After we pondered the data for a while and considered their relationship to other indicators of business activity in our industry, we came to the reluctant conclusion that business was in fact slowing down. This meant we should take a conservative approach to near-term investment— no small matter.

By sharing his base of information with me, the two of us developed a congruent attitude, approach, and conclusion: conservatism in our expansion plans. He left the meeting having decided to scale back growth in his own area of responsibility. I left having decided to share what we had concluded with the business groups I supervised. Thus, this one-on-one produced substantial leverage: the Intel sales manager affected all the other managers who reported to me.

To digress a bit, I also think that one-on-ones at home can help family life. As the father of two teenage daughters, I have found that the conversation in such a time together is very different in tone and kind from what we say to each other in other circumstances. The one-on-one makes each of us take the other seriously and allows subtle and complicated matters to come up for discussion. Obviously, no notes are taken, as father and daughter usually go out for dinner at a restaurant, but a family one-on-one very much resembles a business one-on-one. I strongly recommend both practices.

STAFF MEETINGS

A staff meeting is one in which a supervisor and all of his subordinates participate, and which therefore presents an opportunity for interaction among peers. As we will see later, peer interaction—especially decision-making by a group of peers—is not easy. Yet it is key to good management. The approach to decision-making that we advocate in the next chapter, as well as the workings of the principle of dual reporting (Chapter 9), depend on a group of peers working well together. By learning how this happens in staff meetings, where a group of peers get to know each other, and where the presence of a common supervisor helps peer interaction to develop, managers will be prepared to be members of other working bodies based on peer groups.

Staff meetings also create opportunities for the supervisor to learn from the exchange and confrontation that often develops. In my own case, I get a much better understanding of an issue with which I am not familiar by listening to two people with opposing views discuss it than I do by listening to one side only.

My first experience with staff meetings dates back to my early professional years when I was the head of a small group of engineers doing semiconductor device research. Everyone in this group worked on an isolated aspect of a problem or on a different problem altogether. I was supposed to be the supervisor, but I found that others in the group were often more familiar with the work of another researcher than I was. Thus, a group discussion on any subject tended to get more detailed and more heated, but always more rewarding, than an exchange between me and one other specialist.

What should be discussed at a staff meeting? Anything that affects more than two of the people present. If the meeting degenerates into a conversation between two people working on a problem affecting only them, the supervisor should break it off and move on to something else that will include more of the staff, while suggesting that the two continue their exchange later.

How structured should the meeting be? A free-for-all brainstorming session or controlled with a detailed agenda? It should be mostly controlled, with an agenda issued far enough in advance that the subordinates will have had the chance to prepare their thoughts for the meeting. But it should also include an "open session"— a designated period of time for the staff to bring up anything they want. This is when a varied set of housekeeping matters can be disposed of, as well as when important issues can be given a tentative first look. If it is justified, you can provide time for a more formal discussion about an issue in the scheduled portion of a future meeting.

What is the role of the supervisor in the staff meeting —a leader, observer, expediter, questioner, decision-maker? The answer, of course, is all of them. Please note that lecturer is not listed. A supervisor should never use staff meetings to pontificate, which is the surest way to undermine free discussion and hence the meeting's basic purpose.

The figure opposite shows that the supervisor's most important roles are being a meeting's moderator and facilitator, and controller of its pace and thrust. Ideally, the supervisor should keep things on track, with the

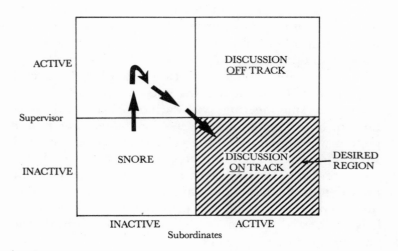

The supervisor's effort at a staff meeting should go into keeping the discussion on track, with the subordinates bearing the brunt of working the issues.

subordinates bearing the brunt of working the issues. Staff meetings are an ideal medium for decision-making, because the group of managers present has typically worked together for a long time. The formal as well as informal authority of each individual has been well established, and everybody knows who likes to spout off, who tends to daydream, who knows what stuff and so on. A staff meeting is like the dinner-table conversation of a family, while other forums of interaction at work, involving people who don't know each other very well, are like a group of strangers having to make a decision together.

OPERATION REVIEWS

This is the medium of interaction for people who don't otherwise have much opportunity to deal with one another. The format here should include formal presentations in which managers describe their work to other managers who are not their immediate supervisors, and to peers in other parts of the company. The basic purpose of an operation review at Intel is to keep the teaching and learning going on between employees several organizational levels apart—people who don't have one-on-ones or staff meetings with each other. This is important for both the junior and senior manager. The junior person will benefit from the comments, criticisms, and suggestions of the senior manager, who in turn will get a different feel for problems from people familiar with their details. Such meetings are also a source of motivation: managers making the presentations will want to leave a good impression on their supervisor's supervisor and on their outside peers.

Who are the players at an operation review? The organizing manager, the reviewing manager, the presenters, and the audience. Each of these players has a distinct role to play if the review is to be a useful one.

The supervisor of the presenting managers—an Intel divisional marketing manager, let's say—should organize the meeting. He should help the presenters decide what issues should be talked about and what should not, what should be emphasized, and what level of detail to go into. The supervisor should also be in charge of housekeeping (the meeting room, visual materials, invitations, and so on). Finally, he should be the timekeeper, scheduling the presentations and keeping them moving along. Though it's hard to judge in advance the time needed for any discussion, the supervisor has presumably had more experience running meetings. In any case, he should pace the presenters using inconspicuous gestures, so that the manager talking doesn't suddenly find himself out of time with only half his points covered.

The reviewing manager is the senior supervisor at whom the review is aimed—like the general manager of an Intel division. He has a very important although more subtle role to play: he should ask questions, make comments, and in general impart the appropriate spirit to the meeting. He is the catalyst needed to provoke audience participation, and by his example he should encourage free expression. He should never preview the material, since that will keep him from reacting spontaneously. Because the senior supervisor is a role model for the junior managers present, he should take his role at the review extremely seriously.

The people presenting the reviews—a group of marketing supervisors, for example—should use visual aids such as overhead transparencies to the extent possible. People are endowed with eyes as well as ears, and the simultaneous use of both definitely helps the audience understand the points being made. But care must be taken, because all too frequently a presenter gets so obsessed with getting through all of his visual material that his message gets lost even while all his charts get flipped. As a rule of thumb, I would recommend four minutes of presentation and discussion time per visual aid, which can include tables, numbers, or graphics. The presenter must highlight whatever he wants to emphasize with a color pen or pointer. Throughout, a presenter has to watch his audience like a hawk. Facial expressions and body language, among other things, will tell him if people are getting the message, if he needs to stop and go over something again, or if he is boring them and should speed up.

The audience at an operation review also has a crucial part to play. One of the distinguishing marks of a good meeting is that the audience participates by asking questions and making comments. If you avoid the presenter's eyes, yawn, or read the newspaper it's worse than not being there at all. Lack of interest undermines the confidence of the presenter. Remember that you are spending a big part of your working day at the review. Make that time as valuable for yourself and your organization as you can. Pay attention and jot down things you've heard that you might try. Ask questions if something is not clear to you and speak up if you can't go along with an approach being recommended. And if a presenter makes a factual error, it is your responsibility to go on record. Remember, you are being *paid to attend* the meeting, which is not meant to be a siesta in the midst of an otherwise busy day. Regard attendance at the meeting for what it is: work.

Mission-Oriented Meetings

Unlike a process-oriented meeting, which is a regularly scheduled affair held to exchange knowledge and information, the mission-oriented meeting is usually held ad hoc and is designed to produce a specific output, frequently a decision. The key to success here is what the *chairman* does. Very often no one is officially given that title, but by whatever name, one person usually has more at stake in the outcome of the meeting than others. In fact, it is usually the chairman or the de facto chairman who calls the meeting, and most of what he contributes should occur before it begins. All too often he shows up as if he were just another attendee and hopes that things will develop as he wants. When a mission-oriented meeting fails to accomplish the purpose for which it was called, the blame belongs to the chairman.

Thus the chairman must have a clear understanding of the meeting's objective—what needs to happen and what decision has to be made. The absolute truth is that if you don't know what you want, you won't get it. So before calling a meeting, ask yourself: What am I trying to accomplish? Then ask, is a meeting necessary? Or desirable? Or justifiable? Don't call a meeting if all the answers aren't yes.

An estimate of the dollar cost of a manager's time,

including overhead, is about $100 per hour. So a meeting involving ten managers for two hours costs the company $2,000. Most expenditures of $2,000 have to be approved in advance by senior people—like buying a copying machine or making a transatlantic trip—yet a manager can call a meeting and commit $2,000 worth of managerial resources at a whim. So even if you're just an invited participant, you should ask yourself if the meeting—and your attendance—is desirable and justified. Tell the chairman—the person who invited you—if you do not feel it is. Determine the purpose of a meeting before committing your time and your company's resources. Get it called off early, at a low-value-added stage, if a meeting makes no sense, and find a less costly way (a one-on-one meeting, a telephone call, a note) to pursue the matter.

Assuming the meeting does need to be held, the chairman faces a set of obligations. The first one has to do with attendance. As the chairman, you must identify who should attend and then try to get those people to come. It is not enough to ask people and hope for the best; you need to follow up and get commitments. If someone invited can't make it himself, see to it that he sends a person with the power to speak for him.

Keep in mind that a meeting called to make a specific decision is hard to keep moving if more than six or seven people attend. Eight people should be the absolute cutoff. Decision-making is not a spectator sport, because onlookers get in the way of what needs to be done.

The chairman is also responsible for maintaining discipline. It is criminal for him to allow people to be late and waste everyone's time. Remember, wasting time here really means that you are wasting the company's money, with the meter ticking away at the rate of $100 per hour per person. Do not worry about confronting the late arriver. Just as you would not permit a fellow employee to steal a piece of office equipment worth $2,000, you shouldn't let anyone walk away with the time of his fellow managers.

The chairman should finally be responsible for logistical matters. He should, for example, make sure that all necessary and audiovisual equipment is present in the meeting room. He should also send out an agenda that clearly states the purpose of the meeting, as well as what role everybody there is expected to play to get the desired output. An example of such an agenda is shown below.

To: Far East Plant Manager
      Manufacturing Manager
      Corporate Construction Manager
      President

From: Far East Construction Manager

Subject: Philippines Plant Location Decision Meeting

Friday, October 1
11:00 a.m.–1:00 p.m.
Santa Clara Conference Room 212
Teleconference connection to Phoenix Conference Room 4
Purpose of meeting: To decide specific location for
Philippine plant expansion

Agenda

11:00–11:30	Manufacturing considerations	(F.E. Plant Manager)
11:30–12:00	Construction considerations	(F.E. Construction Manager)
12:00–12:45	Review of alternatives, including preferred choice	(F.E. Construction Manager)
12:45–1:00	Discussion	(All)

This may sound like too much regimentation for you, but whether it's that or needed discipline depends on your point of view. If the chairman forces you to show up at a meeting prepared and on time, you might consider him a drill sergeant. But if you show up on time, ready to work, and someone else doesn't and isn't, you'll probably begrudge the person responsible for wasting your time. It must be much the same in an operating room. Some people working there may not like a surgeon insisting upon precision, but I am one patient who would much prefer a disciplined operating room to any other kind.

Once the meeting is over, the chairman must nail down exactly what happened by sending out minutes that summarize the discussion that occurred, the decision made, and the actions to be taken. And it's very important that attendees get the minutes quickly, before they forget what happened. The minutes should also be as clear and as specific as possible, telling the reader what is to be done, who is to do it, and when. All this may seem like too much trouble, but if the meeting was worth calling in the first place, the work needed to produce the minutes is a small additional investment (an activity with high leverage) to ensure that the full benefit is obtained from what was done.

Ideally, a manager should never have to call an ad hoc, mission-oriented meeting, because if all runs smoothly, everything is taken care of in regularly scheduled, process-oriented meetings. In practice, however, if all goes well, routine meetings will take care of maybe 80 percent of the problems and issues; the remaining 20 percent will still have to be dealt with in mission-oriented meetings. Remember, Peter Drucker said that if people spend more than 25 percent of their time in meetings, it is a sign of malorganization. I would put it another way: the real sign of malorganization is when people spend more than 25 percent of their time in ad hoc mission-oriented meetings.

5

Decisions,
Decisions

Making decisions—or more properly, participating in
the process by which they are made—is an important and
essential part of every manager's work from one day to
the next. Decisions range from the profound to the trivial, from the complex to the very simple: Should we buy
a building or should we lease it? Issue debt or equity?
Should we hire this person or that one? Should we give
someone a 7 percent or a 12 percent raise? Can we
deposit a phosphosilicate glass with 9 percent phospho-
rus content without jeopardizing its stability in a plastic
package? Can we appeal this case on the basis of Regula-
tion 939 of the Internal Revenue Code? Should we serve
free drinks at our departmental Christmas party?

In traditional industries, where the management chain
of command was precisely defined, a person making a
certain kind of decision was a person occupying a particular position in the organization chart. As the saying
went, authority (to make decisions) went with responsibility (position in the management hierarchy). However,
in businesses that mostly deal with information and
know-how, a manager has to cope with a new phenomenon. Here a rapid divergence develops between power
based on position and power based on knowledge, which

occurs because the base of knowledge that constitutes the foundation of the business changes rapidly.

What do I mean? When someone graduates from college with a technical education, at that time and for the next several years, that young person will be fully up-to-date in the technology of the time. Hence, he possesses a good deal of knowledge-based power in the organization that hired him. If he does well, he will be promoted to higher and higher positions, and as the years pass, his position power will grow but his intimate familiarity with current technology will fade. Put another way, even if today's veteran manager was once an outstanding engineer, he is not now the technical expert he was when he joined the company. At Intel, anyway, we managers get a little more obsolete every day.

So a business like ours has to employ a decision-making process unlike those used in more conventional industries. If Intel used people holding old-fashioned position power to make all its decisions, decisions would be made by people unfamiliar with the technology of the day. And in general, the faster the change in the know-how on which the business depends or the faster the change in customer preferences, the greater the divergence between knowledge and position power is likely to be. If your business depends on what it *knows* to survive and prosper, what decision-making mechanism should you use? The key to success is again the middle manager, who not only is a link in the chain of command but also can see to it that the holders of the two types of power mesh smoothly.

Ideal Model

Illustrated on page 90 is an ideal model of decision-making in a know-how business. The first stage should be *free discussion,* in which all points of view and all aspects of an issue are openly welcomed and debated. The

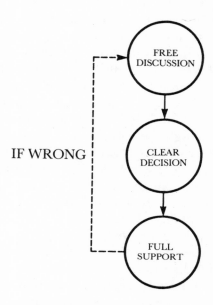

IF WRONG

The ideal decision-making process.

greater the disagreement and controversy, the more important becomes the word *free*. This sounds obvious, but it's not often the practice. Usually when a meeting gets heated, participants hang back, trying to sense the direction of things, saying nothing until they see what view is likely to prevail. They then throw their support behind that view to avoid being associated with a losing position. Bizarre as it may seem, some organizations actually encourage such behavior. Let me quote from a news account relating to the woes of a certain American automobile company: "In the meeting in which I was informed that I was released, I was told, 'Bill, in general, people who do well in this company wait until they hear their superiors express their view and then contribute something in support of that view.' " This is a terrible way to manage. All it produces is bad decisions, because if knowledgeable people withhold opinions, whatever is decided will be based on information and insight less complete than it could have been otherwise.

The next stage is reaching a *clear decision*. Again, the greater the disagreement about the issue, the more important becomes the word *clear*. In fact, particular pains should be taken to frame the terms of the decision with utter clarity. Again, our tendency is to do just the opposite: when we know a decision is controversial we want to obscure matters to avoid an argument. But the argument is not avoided by our being mealy-mouthed, merely postponed. People who don't like a decision will be a lot madder if they don't get a prompt and straight story about it.

Finally, everyone involved must give the decision reached by the group *full support*. This does not necessarily mean agreement: so long as the participants commit to back the decision, that is a satisfactory outcome. Many people have trouble supporting a decision with which they do not agree, but that they need to do so is simply inevitable. Even when we all have the same facts and we all have the interests of an organization in mind, we tend to have honest, strongly felt, real differences of opinion. No matter how much time we may spend trying to forge agreement, we just won't be able to get it on many issues. But an organization does not live by its members agreeing with one another at all times about everything. It lives instead by people committing to support the decisions and the moves of the business. All a manager can expect is that the commitment to support is honestly present, and this is something he can and must get from everyone.

The ideal decision-making model seems an easy one to follow. Yet I have found that it comes easily to only two classes of professional employees—senior managers who have been in the company for a long time, who feel at home with the way things are done, and who identify

with the values of the organization; and the new graduates that we hire, because they used the model as students doing college work. This is the way a team of
students working on a laboratory experiment will resolve
its differences, so for the young engineer the Intel model
is a continuation of what he was used to. But for middle
managers, the decision-making model is easier to accept
intellectually than it is to practice. Why? Because they
often have trouble expressing their views forcefully, a
hard time making unpleasant or difficult decisions, and
an even harder time with the idea that they are expected
to support a decision with which they don't agree. It may
take a while, but the logic of the ideal scheme will eventually win everyone over.

Another desirable and important feature of the model
is that any decision be worked out and reached at the
lowest competent level. The reason is that this is where it will
be made by people who are closest to the situation and
know the most about it. And by "know" I don't just mean
"understand technically." That kind of expertise must
be tempered with judgment, which is developed through
experience and learning from the many errors one has
made in one's career. Thus, ideally, decision-making
should occur in the middle ground, between reliance on
technical knowledge on the one hand, and on the bruises
one has received from having tried to implement and
apply such knowledge on the other. To make a decision,
if you can't find people with both qualities, you should
aim to get the best possible mix of participants available.
For experience, we at Intel are likely to ask a person in
management senior to the other members of the group
to come to the meeting. But it is very important that
everybody there voice opinions and beliefs as *equals*
throughout the free discussion stage, forgetting or ignoring status differentials.

A journalist puzzled by our management style once
asked me, "Mr. Grove, isn't your company's emphasis on

visible signs of egalitarianism such as informal dress, partitions instead of offices, and the absence of other obvious perks like reserved parking spaces, just so much affectation?" My answer was that this is not affectation but a matter of survival. In our business we have to mix knowledge-power people with position-power people daily, and together they make decisions that could affect us for years to come. If we don't link our engineers with our managers in such a way as to get good decisions, we can't succeed in our industry. Now, status symbols most certainly do not promote the flow of ideas, facts, and points of view. What appears to be a matter of style really is a matter of necessity.

The Peer-Group Syndrome

The model is also hard to implement because anybody who makes a business decision also possesses emotions such as pride, ambition, fear, and insecurity. These tend to come to the surface quickly when people who are not used to working with one another are asked to make a decision. This means we need to think about what keeps decision-making from happening smoothly along the lines we've advocated.

The most common problem is something we call the *peer-group syndrome.* A number of years ago, at Intel's very first management training session, we tried some role-playing to show people what can occur when a group of peers meets to solve a problem or make a decision. We sat the people around a table to tackle what was then a live issue for them in their real jobs. Everyone was an organizational equal. The chairman of the meeting was one level higher, but was purposely sent out of the room so he couldn't hear what was to happen. Observers in the audience couldn't believe their eyes and ears as the mock meeting proceeded. The managers working on the problem did nothing but go around in circles for some fifteen minutes, and none of them noticed they weren't getting anywhere. When the chairman was brought back in, he sat down and listened for a while and couldn't believe things either. We watched him lean forward as if he were trying to glean more from the conversation. We then saw a black cloud form over his head; finally he slapped the table and exclaimed, "What's going on here? You people are talking in circles and getting nowhere." After the chairman intervened, the problem was resolved in very short order. We named this the *peer-plus-one* approach, and have used it since then to aid decision-making where we must. Peers tend to look for a more senior manager, even if he is not the most competent or knowledgeable person involved, to take over and shape a meeting.

Why? Because most people are afraid to stick their necks out. This is how John, an Intel software engineer, sees things:

> One of the reasons why people are reluctant to come out with an opinion in the presence of their peers is the fear of going against the group by stating an opinion that is different from that of the group. Consequently, the group as a whole wanders around for a while, feeling each other out, waiting for a consensus to develop before anyone risks taking a position. If and when a group consensus emerges, one of the members will state it *as a group opinion* ("I think *our* position seems to be . . ."), not as a personal position. After a weak statement of the group position, if the rest of the mob buys in, the position becomes more solid and is restated more forcefully.

Note the difference between the situation described earlier by the auto executive and the one John describes. In the former instance, the people were expected to wait for their supervisor to state his opinion first. In the latter, members of the group were waiting for a consensus to develop. The dynamics are different, but the bottom line in both is that people didn't really speak their minds freely. That certainly makes it harder for a manager to make the right decisions.

You can overcome the peer-group syndrome if each of the members has self-confidence, which stems in part from being familiar with the issue under consideration and from experience. But in the end self-confidence mostly comes from a gut-level realization that nobody has ever died from making a wrong business decision, or taking inappropriate action, or being overruled. And everyone in your operation should be made to understand this.

If the peer-group syndrome manifests itself, and the meeting has no formal chairman, the person who has the most at stake should take charge. If that doesn't work, one can always ask the senior person present to assume control. He is likely to be no more expert in the issues at hand than other members of the group—perhaps less expert—but he is likely to act as a godfather, a repository of knowledge about how decisions should be made, and give the group the confidence needed to make a decision.

One thing that paralyzes both knowledge and position power possessors is the fear of simply *sounding dumb*. For the senior person, this is likely to keep him from asking the questions he should ask. The same fear will make other participants merely think their thoughts privately rather than articulate them for all to hear; at best they will whisper what they have to say to a neighbor. As a manager, you should remind yourself that each time an insight or fact is withheld and an appropriate question is suppressed, the decision-making process is less good than it might have been.

A related phenomenon influences lower-level people present in the meeting. This group has to overcome the

fear of being *overruled,* which might mean embarrassment: if the rest of the group or a senior-level manager
vetoed a junior person or opposed a position he was
advocating, the junior manager might lose face in front
of his peers. This, even more than fear of sanctions or
even of the loss of job, makes junior people hang back
and let the more senior people set the likely direction of
decision-making.

But some issues are so complex that those called on to
make a decision honestly aren't really sure how they feel.
When knowledge and position power are separated, the
sense of uncertainty can become especially acute, because the knowledge people are often not comfortable
with the purely business-related factors that might influence a decision. What is often heard is, "We don't know
what the company [or division or department] wants of
us." Similarly, managers holding position power don't
know what to do because they realize they don't know
enough about the technical details to arrive at the correct
decision. We must strive not to be done in by such obsta-
cles. We are all human beings endowed with intelligence
and blessed with willpower. Both can be drawn upon to
help us overcome our fear of sounding dumb or of being
overruled, and lead us to initiate discussion and come
out front with a stand.

Striving for the Output

Sometimes no amount of discussion will produce a consensus, yet the time for a decision has clearly arrived.
When this happens, the senior person (or "peer-plus-
one") who until now has guided, coached, and prodded
the group along has no choice but to make a decision
himself. If the decision-making process has proceeded
correctly up to this point, the senior manager will be
making the decision having had the full benefit of free
discussion wherein all points of view, facts, opinions, and

judgments were aired without position-power prejudice. In other words, it is legitimate—in fact, sometimes unavoidable—for the senior person to wield position-power authority if the clear decision stage is reached and no consensus has developed. It is not legitimate—in fact, it is destructive—for him to wield that authority any earlier. This is often not easy. We Americans tend to be reluctant to exercise position power deliberately and explicitly—it is just "not nice" to give orders. Such reluctance on the part of the senior manager can prolong the first phase of the decision-making process—the time of free discussion—past the optimum point, and the decision will be put off.

If you either enter the decision-making stage too early or wait too long, you won't derive the full benefit of open discussion. The criterion to follow is this: don't push for a decision prematurely. Make sure you have heard and considered the real issues rather than the superficial comments that often dominate the early part of a meeting. But if you feel that you have already heard everything, that all sides of the issue have been raised, it is time to push for a consensus—and failing that, to step in and make a decision. Sometimes free discussion goes on in an unending search for consensus. But, if that happens, people can drift away from the near consensus when they are close to being right, diminishing the chances of reaching the correct decision. So moving on to make the decision at the right time is crucial.

Basically, like other things managers do, decision-making has an *output* associated with it, which in this case is the decision itself. Like other managerial processes, decision-making is likelier to generate high-quality output in a timely fashion if we say clearly at the outset that we expect exactly that. In other words, one of the manager's key tasks is to settle six important questions in advance:

- What decision needs to be made?
- When does it have to be made?
- Who will decide?
- Who will need to be consulted prior to making the decision?
- Who will ratify or veto the decision?
- Who will need to be informed of the decision?

Let me illustrate how these six questions came into play in a recent decision I was involved in. Intel had already decided to expand its Philippine manufacturing plant, roughly doubling its capacity. The next question was where. Only limited space was available next to the existing plant. But, other things being equal, building there was the most desirable thing to do because overhead and communications could be shared, transportation costs between the two plants would amount to virtually nothing, and our employees could be transferred from one plant to the other very easily. The alternative consisted of buying a less expensive plot of land quite some distance away. The land would be not only cheaper but more plentiful, which would allow us to build a relatively inexpensive one- or two-story building. Buying the lot near the existing plant meant that we would have had to build a high-rise to get the amount of floor space we needed, and a high-rise semiconductor manufacturing plant would not be the most efficient. That made us hesitate. But it would be nice to have a second building next to the one we already own. Back and forth and so on and so forth went the discussion.

Let's apply our six questions here. It is clear *what* decision needed to be made: we either build a multistory building next to our existing plant, or we build a one- or two-story building at a new outlying location. As for the question *when:* according to our long-range plans, we needed the new plant in two to two and a half years; if we apply time offsets, we must make the decision within a month. This answers the *when*.

Who will decide? Our facilities/construction people or the Intel group that manages the manufacturing plants? The answer is not easy. The first organization is more sensitive to matters pertaining to the costs and difficulties of construction, and will probably lean toward the new location. The plant management group, knowing that operational benefits will come from having the two plants side by side, will probably opt for the high-rise. So the decision-making body is composed of our construction manager for our Far East locations; his supervisor, the construction manager for the corporation; the manager of the Far East manufacturing plant network; and his supervisor, the senior manufacturing manager. The meeting gave us parallel levels of managers from the two organizations. The sensitivities of two interest groups coming to bear on a single decision is quite common in real corporate life. In such meetings, it is important to give to the two sides roughly equal representation, because only from such balance will an even-handed decision emerge. All of these individuals have consulted their staffs prior to the decision and gathered all relevant knowledge and views on the subject.

Who will ratify or veto the decision? The first common person to whom the senior managers of both organizations report is myself. Also, this was a big enough deal that the president of the company should be involved. Moreover, I was somewhat familiar with the locations in the Philippines and how a plant like the one we have there operates. So I was chosen as the person to veto or ratify the decision of the meeting.

Who will need to be informed of this decision? I chose Gordon Moore, our chairman of the board. He's not directly involved with manufacturing plants like the one contemplated, but we don't build a new one in the Far

East every day, so he should know about what happened.

This is how the decision was made. After studying maps, construction plans and costs, land costs, and traffic patterns, and considering several times everything we thought was important, the group decided to build next to our existing plant but to accept only as much manufacturing area as four stories would yield. The cost would have escalated had we exceeded that. This, with all relevant background, was presented to me at the meeting described on the agenda shown in the previous chapter. I listened to the presentation of the alternatives the group considered and to the reasons why they preferred their choice to these, and after asking a series of questions and probing both the group's information and its thinking process, I ratified the decision. Subsequently I informed Gordon Moore of the outcome, and as you are reading this, the plant is either under construction or already operating.

Employing consistent ways by which decisions are to be made has value beyond simply expediting the decision-making itself. People invest a great deal of energy and emotion in coming up with a decision. Then somebody who has an important say-so or the right to veto it may come across the decision later. If he does veto it, he can be regarded as a Johnny-come-lately who upsets the decision-making applecart. This, of course, will frustrate and demoralize the people who may have been working on it for a long time. If the veto comes as a surprise, however legitimate it may have been on its merits, an impression of political maneuvering is inevitably created. Politics and manipulation or even their appearance should be avoided at all costs. And I can think of no better way to make the decision-making process straightforward than to apply *before the fact* the structure imposed by our six questions.

One last thing. If the final word has to be dramatically different from the expectations of the people who participated in the decision-making process (had I chosen, for example, to cancel the Philippine plant project altogether), make your announcement but don't just walk away from the issue. People need time to adjust, rationalize, and in general put their heads back together. Adjourn, reconvene the meeting after people have had a chance to recover, and solicit their views of the decision at that time. This will help everybody accept and learn to live with the unexpected.

If good decision-making appears complicated, that's because it is and has been for a long time. Let me quote from Alfred Sloan, who spent a lifetime preoccupied with decision-making: "Group decisions do not always come easily. There is a strong temptation for the leading officers to make decisions themselves without the sometimes onerous process of discussion." Because the process is indeed onerous, people sometimes try to run away from it. A middle manager I once knew came straight from one of the better business schools and possessed what we might call a "John Wayne" mentality. Having become frustrated with the way Intel made decisions, he quit. He joined a company where his employers assured him during the interview that people were encouraged to make individual decisions which they were then free to implement. Four months later, he came back to Intel. He explained that if he could make decisions without consulting anybody, so could everybody else.

6

Planning:
Today's Actions for
Tomorrow's Output

The Planning Process

Most people think "planning" is one of the loftier responsibilities of management—we all learned somewhere that "a manager plans, organizes, controls." In
fact, planning is an ordinary everyday activity; it's something all of us do all the time with no fanfare, in both our
personal and professional lives. For instance, as you're
driving to work in the morning, you are likely to decide
whether or not you need gasoline. You look at the gauge
to see how much gas you have in the tank, you estimate
how far it is you need to go, and you then make a rough
guess as to how much gas you need to get to and from
your office. By comparing in your mind the gas you need
with the gas you have, you decide whether you should
stop for gas or not. This is a simple example of planning.

The dynamics of planning can best be understood by
going back to our basic production principles. As we
learned in Chapter 2, the key method of controlling the
future output of a factory is through the use of a system
of forecasting demand and building to forecast. We oper-
ated our factory to fill existing and anticipated orders.

Our job was to match the factory's output at a given time with the orders for it. If the projected output did not match the projected market demand, either we made additional production starts or we reduced them to eliminate the excess. How one plans at the factory can then be summarized as follows: step 1, determine the market demand for product; step 2, establish what the factory will produce if no adjustment is made; and step 3, reconcile the projected factory output with the projected market demand by adjusting the production schedule.

Your general planning process should consist of analogous thinking. Step 1 is to establish projected need or demand: What will the environment demand from you, your business, or your organization? Step 2 is to establish your present status: What are you producing now? What will you be producing as your projects in the pipeline are completed? Put another way, where will your business be if you do nothing different from what you are now doing? Step 3 is to compare and reconcile steps 1 and 2. Namely, what more (or less) do you need to do to produce what your environment will demand?

Let's consider each step in more detail.

STEP 1—ENVIRONMENTAL DEMAND

Just what is your environment? If you look at your own group within an organization as if it were a stand-alone company, you see that your environment is made up of other such groups that directly influence what you do. For example, if you were the manager of the company's mailroom, your environment would consist of customers who need your services (the rest of the company), vendors who are able to provide you with certain capabilities (postage meters, mail carts), and finally, your competitors. You don't, of course, have competitors internally— but you can compare your service to one like United

Parcel as a way to judge performance and set standards.

What should you look for when you examine your environment? You should attempt to determine your customers' expectations and their perception of your performance. You should keep abreast of technological developments like electronic mail and other alternative ways of doing your job. You should evaluate the performance of your vendors. You should also evaluate the performance of other groups in the organization to which you belong. Does some other group (like the traffic department) affect how well you can do your work? Can that group meet your needs?

Once you have established what constitutes your environment, you need to examine it in two time frames— now, and sometime in the future, let's say in a year. The questions then become: What do my customers want from me now? Am I satisfying them? What will they expect from me one year from now? You need to focus on the difference between what your environment demands from you now and what you expect it to demand from you a year from now. Such a *difference analysis* is crucial, because if your current activities satisfy the current demands placed on your business, anything more and new should be undertaken to match this difference. How you *react* to this difference is in fact the key outcome of the planning process.

Should you at this stage consider what practical steps you can actually take to handle matters? No, that will just confuse the issue. What would happen to a factory, for instance, if the marketing organization adjusted its demand forecast on the basis of its own assessment of the manufacturing unit's ability to deliver? If marketing knew they could sell 100 widgets per month but thought that manufacturing could only deliver ten, and so submitted a demand forecast of ten units, manufacturing would never tool up to satisfy the *real* demand.

STEP 2—PRESENT STATUS

The second step of planning is to determine your present status. You do this by listing your present capabilities and the projects you have in the works. As you account for them, be sure to use the same terms, or "currency," in which you stated demand. For instance, if your demand is listed in terms of completed product designs, your work-in-process should be listed as partially completed product designs. You also need to look at timing; namely, when will these projects come out of your "pipeline"? You must ask yourself, will every project now moving through be completed? Chances are, no, some will get scrapped or aborted, and you have to factor this into your forecasted output. Statistically, in semiconductor manufacturing, only some 80 percent of the material started actually gets finished. Similarly, while it is impossible to be precise in every case, it is prudent to factor in some percentage of loss for managerial projects as well.

STEP 3—WHAT TO DO TO CLOSE THE GAP

The final step of planning consists of undertaking new tasks or modifying old ones to close the gap between your environmental demand and what your present activities will yield. The first question is, What do you *need* to do to close the gap? The second is, What *can* you do to close the gap? Consider each question separately, and then decide what you actually will do, evaluating *what* effect your actions will have on narrowing the gap, and *when.* The set of actions you decide upon is your *strategy.*

Much confusion exists between what is strategy and what is tactics. Although the distinction is rarely of practical significance, here's one that might be useful. As you formulate in words what you plan to do, the most abstract and general summary of those actions meaningful to you is your strategy. What you'll do to implement the strategy is your tactics. Frequently, a strategy at one managerial level is the tactical concern of the next higher level. Let's return to our mailroom. Assume that the manager of corporate communications has decided to install electronic mail service between all manufacturing plants. This is his strategy—a plan of action to improve communications capability between plants. The mailroom manager then has to do certain things to provide service when electronic mail equipment is put in place. For instance, his strategy may be to install printers in the mailroom and set up a service to deliver printed copies throughout the building. The mailroom manager's strategy is the communications manager's tactics.

SOME EXAMPLES

As he defined his present environment and status, Bruce, an Intel marketing manager, found that he had only three people in his department who could possibly handle a huge inventory of projects. As he looked at his desired future status, he concluded that every single one of the projects had to be completed. Not finishing everything would result in significant extra cost and far more effort later. Bruce was faced with a genuine dilemma, especially since the budget kept him from hiring more people. He realized that the best he could do was to narrow the gap a bit—getting the projects and his group's capacity to complete them to converge. A complete match was impossible.

Bruce decided to move as many noncritical tasks as possible to other groups in the company—groups less qualified for them than his own but also less busy. He also made arrangements with his manager to bring a summer student on board to help with some easily definable tasks, and then set himself up to monitor the performance of his group tightly. He also proceeded to look at other avenues that could help him in the longer term, such as splitting the job of completing some of the work with other similar marketing groups in the company and eliminating any duplication of effort between them. Finally Bruce initiated a request to increase the size of his organization. His plan—and the obvious reality that full convergence between his tasks and his capabilities was not possible even after going the extra mile—would lay the basis for his request.

Let's illustrate with another example. Our middle manager Cindy, the manufacturing process engineer whom we've met before, is responsible for maintaining and improving the process by which complex microchips are produced in a plant. She defines her environment as a collection of "objects" and "influences." The "objects" are new processes and manufacturing tools that have not yet been tested in production. The "influences" are the people who can affect her work directly or indirectly. Development engineers, for example, would like her to require *less* experimentation and documentation before she chooses to implement new processes they have developed. Meanwhile, production engineers would like her to provide *more* experimentation and documentation on these same new processes. And finally, there are the product engineers eager to get chips out the door who need her help to do that, along with other members of the production team who put pressure on her to ensure that the new processes are manufacturable and the new manufacturing tools work as soon as they are put to use. Cindy herself works like a consultant, advising each group influencing her about whether something can go into production—the chief coordinator for the set of events required to put a product, a process, or a tool on stream. Her "customer" is the production area itself, and her "vendors" are the engineering groups from production, development, and product engineering.

Analyzing her present status, Cindy found that the data and experimentation she needed from the development group always came in incomplete. Looking into matters further, she found that providing complete data and adhering to schedules were not really high on the development engineers' set of priorities. Determining where she needed to go, it was clear to Cindy that she must have all future new processes and production machinery tested, debugged, demonstrated, and, most important, accompanied by the necessary data for them to be accepted and used by the production engineers, who had become more demanding because of past problems.

Cindy then defined her strategy—her plan of action—to get there. She specified exactly what steps had to be completed before any new process was to be implemented or tool deployed. Then she used time offsets (remember the breakfast factory) to determine when each step needed to be done in order for her entire plan to be completed on time. Next, she got the manager of the development engineers to agree to her detailed schedule. She negotiated with him what she had to do and what they had to do—and by what date—in order to meet what became the mutually agreed-upon goals. Finally, to ensure that she stayed on track, she decided to monitor all of her "vendors" on a weekly basis. She would also publish their performance against the schedule to motivate them to meet key dates (an indicator) and to tell her about potential problems (a window in the black box).

The Output of the Planning Process

The key to both Bruce's and Cindy's efforts is that their planning produced tasks that had to be performed *now* in order to affect *future* events. I have seen far too many people who upon recognizing today's gap try very hard to determine what decision has to be made to close it. But today's gap represents a failure of planning sometime in the past. By analogy, forcing ourselves to concentrate on the decisions needed to fix today's problem is like scurrying after our car has already run out of gas. Clearly we should have filled up earlier. To avoid such a fate, remember that as you plan you must answer the question: What do I have to do *today* to solve—or better, avoid—*tomorrow's* problem?

Thus, the true output of the planning process is the set of tasks it causes to be implemented. The output of Intel's annual plan, for instance, is the actions taken and changes prompted as a result of the thinking process that took place throughout the organization. I, for one, hardly ever look at the bound volume finally called the Annual Plan. In other words, the output of the planning process is the *decisions* made and the *actions* taken as a result of the process.

How far ahead should the planners look? At Intel, we put ourselves through an annual strategic long-range planning effort in which we examine our future five years off. But what is really being influenced here? It is the *next year*—and only the next year. We will have another chance to replan the second of the five years in the next year's long-range planning meeting, when that year will become the first year of the five. So, keep in mind that you implement only that portion of a plan that lies within the time window between now and the next time you go through the exercise. Everything else you can look at again. We should also be careful not to plan too frequently, allowing ourselves time to judge the impact of the decisions we made and to determine whether our decisions were on the right track or not. In other words, we need the feedback that will be indispensable to our planning the next time around.

Who should be involved in the planning process? The operating management of the organization. Why? Be-

cause the idea that planners can be people apart from
those implementing the plan simply does not work. Plan-
✓ ning cannot be made a separate career but is instead a
key managerial activity, one with enormous leverage
through its impact on the future performance of an organization. But this leverage can only be realized through
a marriage, and a good collaborative one at that, between planning and implementation.

✓   Finally, remember that by saying "yes"—to projects, a
course of action, or whatever—you are implicitly saying
"no" to something else. Each time you make a commitment, you forfeit your chance to commit to something
else. This, of course, is an inevitable, inescapable consequence of allocating any finite resource. People who plan
have to have the guts, honesty, and discipline to drop
projects as well as to initiate them, to shake their heads
"no" as well as to smile "yes."

*Management by Objectives: The Planning Process Applied to
Daily Work*

The system of management by objectives assumes that
because our concerns here are short-range, we should
know quite well what our environment demands from us.
Thus, management by objectives—MBO—concentrates
on steps 2 and 3 of the planning process and tries very
hard to make them specific. The idea behind MBO is
extremely simple: If you don't know where you're going,
you will not get there. Or, as an old Indian saying puts
it, "If you don't know where you're going, any road will
get you there."

A successful MBO system needs only to answer two
questions:

  1. Where do I want to go? (The answer provides the
  objective.)

2. How will I pace myself to see if I am getting there? (The answer gives us milestones, or *key results*.)

To illustrate an objective and a key result, consider the following: I want to go to the airport to catch a plane in an hour. That is my objective. I know that I must drive through towns A, B, and C on my way there. My key results become reaching A, B, and C in 10, 20, and 30 minutes respectively. If I have been driving for 20 minutes and haven't yet made town A, I know I'm lost. Unless I get off the highway and ask someone for directions, I probably won't make my flight.

Upon what time period should an MBO system focus? MBO is largely designed to provide feedback relevant to the specific task at hand; it should tell us *how* we are doing so we can make adjustments in *whatever* we are doing if need be, such as getting off the highway and asking for directions. For the feedback to be effective, it must be received very soon after the activity it is measuring occurs. Accordingly, an MBO system should set objectives for a relatively short period. For example, if we plan on a yearly basis, the corresponding MBO system's time frame should be at least as often as quarterly or perhaps even monthly.

The one thing an MBO system should provide par excellence is focus. This can only happen if we keep the number of objectives small. In practice, this is rare, and here, as elsewhere, we fall victim to our inability to say "no"—in this case, to too many objectives. We must realize—and act on the realization—that if we try to focus on everything, we focus on nothing. A few extremely well-chosen objectives impart a clear message about what we say "yes" to and what we say "no" to— which is what we must have if an MBO system is to work.

TWO CASE HISTORIES

To familiarize ourselves with the MBO system, let's look at a case history, Columbus' discovery of the New World, though how I tell the story takes considerable liberties with the grammar-school version of the event. Thanks to its annual planning process of 1491, the government of Spain concluded that it could not continue a war everybody felt was utterly necessary unless money became available to buy weapons and ammunition. Since pushing the Moors out of Spain was the supreme goal of Queen Isabella's government, the Queen needed the funds to do it. Isabella decided she would get money by dramatically improving Spain's foreign trade balance. She then talked to her subordinate—Christopher Columbus—and told him about her objective. Columbus agreed to think about various ways to do what she wanted and after a time went back to her with several suggestions, which included finding pirate-free passage to England and perhaps finding a new route to the Orient. Isabella and Columbus discussed the entire matter freely, eventually reaching a clear decision that he would look for a new route to the East.

Once the decision was made, Columbus began to think of all the things that he would need to do to accomplish his intent. In MBO terms, the Queen defined *her* own objective (increase Spain's wealth); Columbus and the Queen then agreed upon *his* objective (find a new route to the Orient). Columbus then went on to formulate the key results by which he would pace himself, which included obtaining several ships, training crews, conducting a shakedown cruise, setting sail, and so forth, with each possessing a specific deadline.

The relationship between Isabella's and Columbus' objectives is clear. The Queen wanted to increase her nation's wealth, while Columbus wanted to find a safe trade route to the Orient. And we see a nesting hierarchy of objectives: if the subordinate's objectives are met, the supervisor's will be as well.

Now, the key results can come in like clockwork, but the objectives can still be missed. For Columbus, the key results were relatively easy to achieve, but he most certainly did not find a new trade route to China, and therefore failed to meet his objective.

Did Columbus perform well even though he failed by strict MBO terms? He did discover the New World, and that was a source of incalculable wealth for Spain. So it is entirely possible for a subordinate to perform well and be rated well even though he missed his specified objective. The MBO system is meant to pace a person—to put a stopwatch in his own hand so he can gauge his own performance. It is not a legal document upon which to base a performance review, but should be just one input used to determine how well an individual is doing. If the supervisor mechanically relies on the MBO system to evaluate his subordinate's performance, or if the subordinate uses it rigidly and forgoes taking advantage of an emerging opportunity because it was not a specified objective or key result, then both are behaving in a petty and unprofessional fashion.

Let's illustrate the workings of the MBO system using the decision about Intel's plant expansion in the Philippines. The Far East construction manager had an objective that read "Obtain decision on Philippine plant expansion." The key results supporting the objective were: 1) Do a study of land availability near the present plant and at other acceptable locations by June. 2) Do financial analyses showing the trade-offs between land costs and construction costs, as well as the operating costs associated with the two locations. 3) Present the results to the plant location steering group, and obtain a decision from them. 4) Have Grove ratify the decision by October.

Each key result was accomplished and the objective

was met. Note that the objective is relatively short-range and the key results are so specific that a person knows without question whether he has completed them and done it on time or not. Accordingly, to be useful a key result must contain very specific wording and dates, so that when deadline time arrives, there is no room for ambiguity.

As you might have guessed, the Far East construction manager's supervisor had an objective that read "Ensure that all plant expansion projects stay on schedule." To support this objective he in turn had a key result, much like his subordinate's *objective,* that said "Obtain Philippine plant expansion decision by October."

You can now see, I hope, the parallels between how Isabella's government and Intel work. A manager's objectives are supported by an appropriate set of key results. His objectives in turn are tied to his supervisor's objectives so that if the manager meets his objectives, his supervisor will meet his. But the MBO system cannot be run mechanically by a computer. The system requires judgment and common sense to set the hierarchy of objectives and the key results that support them. Both judgment and common sense are also required when using MBO to guide you in your work from one day to the next.

Part Three

TEAM
OF
TEAMS

7

The
Breakfast Factory
Goes National

We left the breakfast factory as it was enjoying great success—so great, in fact, that we had to install a continuous egg-boiling unit at considerable expense. The equipment produced breakfasts of unprecedented uniformity. Moreover, our volume grew to the point where we could use the egg-boiling unit at full capacity; hence, our cost of delivering outstanding breakfasts steadily declined. We passed on some of the savings to our customers, and soon the reputation of our breakfasts spread.

Like good entrepreneurs, we knew we had a good thing going and started another branch of the Breakfast Factory across town (we even named it that). This too became a remarkable success. Soon thereafter *Neighborhood Gourmet,* a magazine with a large national circulation, ran a story on our operation. We decided to seize the opportunity and franchise the Breakfast Factory nationwide. We rapidly moved into neighborhoods with the right demographic mix for our breakfasts, and we were soon enough running a vast network of Breakfast Factories.

Before long we found, however, that the network required a set of tasks and skills very different from those needed to run our one restaurant. The most important of these was to figure out how to use the advantages made possible by having a local entrepreneur set up and run each franchise without losing the enormous economies of scale that became available to us. Because the local manager knows his neighborhood, he can adapt his operation to it and so, we hope, operate the most profitable franchise possible. At the same time, with over a hundred Breakfast Factories, our purchasing power is immense. If we centralize certain activities, we are in a position to do many things much better and much less expensively than each of our franchises could do individually. And most important, because the quality of our breakfasts has played a major role in our success so far, we have to be very concerned about maintaining a perception of first-rate food and service. In other words, we could not permit any one Breakfast Factory branch or those in any region to jeopardize the real secret of our business.

In fact, the centralization-decentralization dichotomy is so pervasive that it has become one of the most important themes in the management of our network. Do we, for instance, want to advertise locally or nationally? Do we want to give the local manager the control over advertising in his community? We don't know who reads the *Daily Blatt,* and he probably does. Do we want to give him the right to hire and fire personnel? Should we let him set his wage scale, or do we want to impose one nationally? The latter hardly makes sense, since labor market conditions vary considerably from region to region. But we do want to buy our sophisticated automatic machinery centrally. After all, it has taken us a long time to develop suitable vendors and the capacity to test the incoming machines given our demanding requirements. We now have a sizable group of people doing only that in Chicago, and we hardly want each branch or even each region to duplicate the effort.

But I don't think we should buy all our eggs in Chicago. We want them to be fresh, and we don't want to truck this delicate commodity all over the country. Neither do we want to have each branch set up its own incoming egg inspection operation. Here some kind of compromise makes sense, such as regional egg purchasing centers, with each only a few hours by truck from all the franchise locations in the region. We do want uniform, high-quality standards everywhere and we will monitor each of the franchises to make sure that they are adhered to. In other words, we definitely want to impose national quality control standards.

What about items on the menu? By and large we want to keep the same core menu everywhere—people going into the Breakfast Factory should be able to count on some basic choices. But we should also recognize regional differences in culinary taste, so some discretion ought to be left to the individual franchises.

What about real estate? Should we allow our Breakfast Factories to be housed in any locally available building? Or should we prescribe a uniform construction style and build each of them from the ground up? Perhaps we should go with whatever building is available provided it meets some standards we set in Chicago.

What about furniture? Does it have to be utterly uniform? Should Chicago buy furniture for all branches? What about tableware? Since people tend to associate what they eat with and from with the breakfast, we should probably use the same tableware all over the country, which means we might as well purchase all that at one place too. But it is ridiculous for a local operation in Montana to requisition Chicago for a few broken plates. So we should probably have a couple of regional warehouses from which tableware could be delivered quickly.

How do we choose the location of new franchises within each metropolitan area? Should we make the decisions in Chicago? Should I decide as the CEO of the Breakfast Factory Corporation or should the corporate

staff let the local branch manager decide? Or perhaps
Chicago should decide after consulting with the regional
managers, who, after all, know their own areas better
than my staff and I do.

Things have become very complicated. Sometimes as
I sit behind my big desk at corporate headquarters, I
wish I could go back to the early days when I was getting
the eggs and toast and pouring the coffee myself. Or if
not that, at least back to the days when I was running a
single Breakfast Factory, and I knew everybody by name
and could make all the decisions without having to struggle with a mountain of pros and cons. Then there was
virtually no overhead. Now there's a corporate personnel manager. There's also a traffic manager, who wants
to buy a computer to optimize the flow of eggs from the
regional centers to the individual franchises. He says he
can minimize transportation costs while ensuring same-
day delivery. He also claims that if he had this computer,
he could keep the tableware inventory at the lowest possible level. It won't be long before we'll have a corporate
manager for real estate acquisitions. Very complicated
indeed.

Earlier, we established the fact that the game of management is a team game: a manager's output is the output of the organizations under his supervision or influence. We now discover that management is not just a
team game, it is a game in which we have to fashion a
team of teams, where the various individual teams exist
in some suitable and mutually supportive relationship
with each other.

8
Hybrid Organizations

What happened to the Breakfast Factory has to happen, or has already happened, to every reasonably large organization.

Most middle managers run departments that are a part of a larger organization. The "black boxes" they oversee are connected to other black boxes in much the same way that the Breakfast Factories are linked to each other and to the main office. So let us look more carefully at what happens within an organization composed of smaller units.

Though most are mixed, organizations can come in two extreme forms: in totally *mission-oriented* form or in totally *functional* form. The Breakfast Factory Corporation could be organized in one or the other extreme form, as shown on the next page. In the mission-oriented organization (a), which is completely decentralized, each individual business unit pursues what it does—its mission—with little tie-in to other units. Here, each Breakfast Factory is responsible for all elements of its operation: determining its own location and constructing its own building, doing its own merchandising, acquiring and maintaining its own personnel, and doing its own purchasing. In the end it submits monthly financial state-

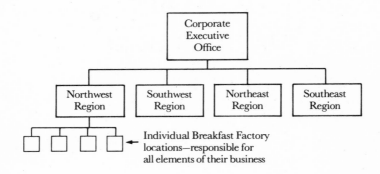

a.

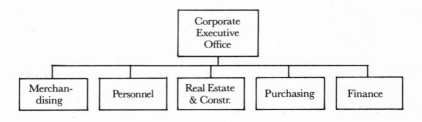

All responsible for their respective activities at all branch locations

b.

The Breakfast Factory network organized in (a) totally mission-oriented and (b) totally functional forms.

ments to the corporate executive office.

At the other extreme is the totally functional organization (b), which is completely centralized. In a Breakfast Factory Corporation set up this way, the merchandising department is responsible for merchandising at *all* locations; the staff of the personnel organization hires, fires, and evaluates personnel at *all* branches; and so on.

The desire to give the individual branch manager the power to respond to local conditions moves us toward a mission-oriented organization. But a similarly legitimate desire to take advantage of the obvious economies of scale and to increase the leverage of the expertise we have in each operational area across the entire corporation would push us toward a functional organization. In the real world, of course, we look for a compromise between the two extremes. In fact, the search for the appropriate compromise has preoccupied managers for a long, long time. Alfred Sloan summed up decades of experience at General Motors by saying, "Good management rests on a reconciliation of centralization and decentralization." Or, we might say, on a balancing act to get the best combination of responsiveness and leverage.

Let's now look at Intel's organization form, as shown on the next page. We are a *hybrid* organization. Our hybrid nature comes from the fact that the form of the overall corporate organization results from a mix of the business divisions, which are mission-oriented, and the functional groups. This is much like the way I imagine any army is organized. The business divisions are analogous to individual fighting units, which are provided with blankets, paychecks, aerial surveillance, intelligence, and so forth by the functional organizations, which supply such services to all fighting units. Because each such unit does not have to maintain its own support groups, it can concentrate on a specific mission, like taking a hill in a battle. And for that, each unit has all the necessary freedom of action and independence.

The functional groups can be viewed as if they were internal subcontractors. Let's take a sales organization as an example. Though a lot of companies use outside sales representatives, an internal group presumably provides the service at less expense and with greater responsiveness. Likewise, manufacturing, finance, or data processing can all be regarded as functional groups, which, as

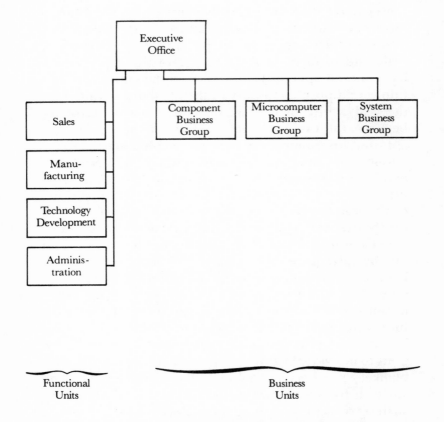

Intel is a hybrid organization: balancing to get the best combination of responsiveness and leverage.

internal subcontractors, provide services to all the business units.

Some two thirds of Intel's employees work in the functional units, indicating their enormous importance. What are some of the advantages of organizing so much of the company in such groups? The first is the economies of scale that can be achieved. Take the case of computerized information processing. Complex com-

puter equipment is very expensive, and the capacity of
large electronic machines can be best used if all the various business units draw from them. If each unit had its
own computer, very expensive equipment would be sitting idle much of the time. Another important advantage
is that resources can be shifted and reallocated to respond to changes in corporate-wide priorities. For instance, because manufacturing is organized functionally,
we can change the mix of product being made to match
need as perceived by the entire corporation. If each business unit did its own manufacturing, shifting capacity
away from one unit to another would be a cumbersome
and sticky exercise. And the advantage here is that the
expertise of specialists—know-how managers, such as
the research engineers who work in technology development—can be applied across the breadth of the entire
corporation, giving their knowledge and work enormous
leverage. Finally, Intel's functional groups allow the
business units to concentrate on mastering their specific
trades rather than having to worry about computers,
production, technology, and so forth.

Having so much of Intel organized in functional units
also has its disadvantages. The most important is the
information overload hitting a functional group when it
must respond to the demands made on it by diverse and
numerous business units. Even conveying needs and demands often becomes very difficult—a business unit has
to go through a number of management layers to influence decision-making in a functional group. Nowhere is
this more evident than in the negotiations that go on to
secure a portion of centralized—and limited—resources
of the corporation, be it production capacity, computer
time, or space in a shared building. Indeed, things often
move beyond negotiation to intense and open competition among business units for the resources controlled
by the functional groups. The bottom line here is that
both the negotiation and competition waste time and

energy because neither contributes to the output or the general good of the company.

What are some of the advantages of organizing much of a company in a mission-oriented form? There is only one. It is that the individual units can stay in touch with the needs of their business or product areas and initiate changes rapidly when those needs change. *That is it.* All other considerations favor the functional-type of organization. But the business of any business is to respond to the demands and needs of its environment, and the need to be responsive is so important that it always leads to much of any organization being grouped in mission-oriented units.

Countless managers have tried to find the best mix of the two organizational forms. And it's been no different at Intel, among senior management and throughout the ranks of hundreds of middle managers, who from time to time attempt to improve the organization of the groups they supervise. But no matter how many times we have examined possible organizational forms, we have always concluded that there is simply no alternative to the hybrid organizational structure.

So that is how Intel is organized today. To further my case that hybrid organizations are inevitable, consider a press release that I read recently. One of dozens that show up in the weekly trade newspapers, it is reproduced here with only the names changed.

ABC TECHNOLOGIES REALIGNS

(SANTA CLARA, CA) Three-year-old ABC Technologies, Inc., has reorganized into three product divisions. The Super System Division Vice President and General Manager is John Doe, formerly Vice President and Engineering Director and a company founder. Vice President and General Manager of the Ultra System Division is former Sales and Marketing Vice President William Smith. Vice President and

General Manager of the Hyper System Division is Robert Worker, formerly Manager of Product Design.

All three division heads report to ABC Technologies President and Chief Executive Samuel Simon. The divisions will have product marketing and product development responsibilities, while sales and manufacturing responsibilities will remain at the corporate level under newly named Sales Vice President Albert Abel and Manufacturing Vice President William Weary.

Note how the change follows the pattern we outlined and analyzed. As the company grew and its product line broadened, the number of things it had to keep track of multiplied. It made more and more sense to create an organization serving each product line; hence the three product divisions. But as the news release indicates, the major functional organizations of ABC Technologies, such as sales and manufacturing, will remain centralized and will serve the three mission-oriented organizations.

Here I would like to propose Grove's Law: *All large organizations with a common business purpose end up in a hybrid organizational form.*

The Breakfast Factory, an army, Intel, and ABC Technologies provide examples. But just about *every* large company or enterprise that I know is organized in a hybrid form. Take an educational institution in which one finds individual mission-oriented departments such as mathematics, English, engineering, and so on, and also administration, composed of personnel, security, and library services, whose combined task is to supply the common resources that each of the individual departments needs to function.

Another very different example of the hybrid form can be found in the national Junior Achievement organization. Here each individual chapter runs its own business, with each deciding what product to sell, actually selling it, and otherwise maintaining all aspects of the business. Nevertheless, the national organization controls the way the chapters are to go about their own pursuits: the form in which the individual businesses are to be structured, the paperwork requirements, and the rewards for successful operation.

The use of the hybrid organizational form does not even necessarily depend on how large a business or activity is. A friend of mine is a lawyer in a medium-size law firm. He told me how his firm tried to deal with the problems and conflicts he and his colleagues were having over resources they all shared, such as the steno pool and office space. They ended up forming an executive committee that would not interfere with the legal (mission-oriented) work of the individual attorneys but would address the acquisition and allocation of common, shared resources. Here is a small operation finding itself with the hybrid organizational form.

Do any exceptions exist to the universality of hybrid organizations? The only exceptions that come to my mind are conglomerates, which are typically organized in a totally mission-oriented form. Why are they an exception to our rule? Because they do not have a common business purpose. The various divisions (or companies) in this case are all independent and bear no relationship to one another beyond the conglomerate profit and loss statement. But within each business unit of the conglomerate, the organization is likely to be structured along the hybrid line.

Of course, each hybrid organization is unique because a limitless number of points lie between the hypothetical extremes of the totally functional and the totally mission-oriented forms. In fact, a single organization may very well shift back and forth between the two poles, movement that should be brought on by pragmatic considerations. For example, a company with an inadequate computer acquires a large, powerful new one, making possible centralized economies of scale. Conversely, a company replaces a large computer with small inexpensive ones that can be readily installed in various mission-oriented units without loss of the economies of scale. This is how a business can adapt. But the most important consideration should be this: the shift back and forth between the two types of organizations can and should be initiated to match the operational styles and aptitudes of the managers running the individual units.

As I've said, sooner or later all reasonably large companies must cope with the problems inherent in the workings of a hybrid organization. The most important task before such an organization is the optimum and timely allocation of its resources and the efficient resolution of conflicts arising over that allocation.

Though this problem may be very complex, "allocators" working out of some central office are certainly not the answer. In fact, the most glaring example of inefficiency I've encountered went on some years ago in Hungary, where I once lived and where a central planning organization decided what goods were to be produced, when, and where. The rationale for such planning was very solid, but in practice it usually fell far, far short of meeting real consumer needs. In Hungary I was an amateur photographer. During the winter, when I needed high-contrast film, none was to be found anywhere. Yet during the summer, everyone was up to his waist in the stuff, even though regular film was in short supply. Year after year, decision-making in the central planning organization was so clumsy that it could not even respond to totally predictable changes in demand. In our business culture, the allocation of shared resources and the reconciliation of the conflicting needs and desires of the independent business units are theoretically the function of corporate management. Practically, however, the transaction load is far too heavy to be handled in one place. If we at Intel tried to resolve all conflicts and allocate all resources at the top, we would begin to resemble the group that ran the Hungarian economy.

Instead, the answer lies with middle managers. Within a company, they are, in the first place, numerous enough to cover the entire range of operation; and, in the second place, very close to the problem we're talking about—namely, generating internal resources and consuming those resources. For middle managers to succeed at this high-leverage task, two things are necessary. First, they must accept the inevitability of the hybrid organizational form if they are to serve its workings. Second, they must develop and master the practice through which a hybrid organization can be managed. This is *dual reporting,* the subject of our next chapter.

9

Dual
Reporting

To put a man on the moon, NASA asked several major contractors and many subcontractors to work together, each on a different aspect of the project. An unintended consequence of the moon shot was the development of a new organizational approach: *matrix management.* This provided the means through which the work of various contractors could be coordinated and managed so that if problems developed in one place, they did not subvert the entire schedule. Resources could be diverted, for example, from a strong organization to one that was slipping in order to help the latter make up lost time.

Matrix management is a complicated affair. Books have been written about it and entire courses of instruction devoted to it. But the core idea was that a project manager, somebody outside any of the contractors involved, could wield as much influence on the work of units within a given company as could the company management itself. Thus, NASA elaborated the principle of dual reporting on a grand scale. In reality, the basic idea had been quietly at work for many years, enabling hybrid organizations of all types to function, from the neighborhood high school to Alfred Sloan's General Motors—not to mention the Breakfast Factory franchises. Let's re-create how Intel came to adopt a dual reporting system.

Where Should Plant Security Report?

When our company was young and small, we stumbled onto dual reporting almost by accident. At a staff meeting we were trying to decide to whom the security personnel at our new outlying plants should report. We had two choices. One would have the employees report to the plant manager. But a plant manager, by background, is typically an engineer or a manufacturing person who knows very little about security issues and cares even less. The other choice would have them report to the security manager at the main plant. He hired them in the first place, and he is the expert who sets the standards that the security officers are supposed to adhere to throughout the company. And it was clear that security procedures and practices at the outlying plants had to conform to some kind of corporate standard.

There was only one problem with the latter arrangement. The security manager works at corporate headquarters and not at the outlying plant, so how would he know if the security personnel outside the main plant even showed up, or came in late, or otherwise performed badly? He wouldn't. After we wrestled with the dilemma for a while, it occurred to us that perhaps security personnel should report *jointly* to the corporate security manager *and* to the local plant manager. The first would specify how the job ought to be done, and the second would monitor how it was being performed day by day.

While the arrangement seemed to solve both problems, the staff couldn't quite accept it. We found ourselves asking, "A person has to have a boss, so who is in charge here?" Could an employee in fact have two bosses? The answer was a tentative "yes," and the culture of joint reporting relationships, dual reporting, was born. It was a slow, laborious birth.

But the need for dual reporting is actually quite fundamental. Let's think for a minute about how a manager comes to be. The first step in his career is being an individual contributor—a salesman, for instance. If he proves himself a superior salesman, he is promoted to the position of sales manager, where he supervises people in his functional specialty, sales. When he has shown himself to be a superstar sales manager he is promoted again, this time becoming a regional sales manager. If he works at Intel, he is now not only supervising salesmen but also so-called field application engineers, who obviously know more about technical matters than he does but whom he still manages. The promotions continue until our superstar finds himself a general manager of a business division. Among other things, our new general manager has no experience with manufacturing. So while he is perfectly capable of supervising his manufacturing manager in the more general aspects of his job, the new boss has no choice but to leave the technical aspects to his subordinate, because as a graduate of sales, he has absolutely no background in manufacturing. In other divisions of the corporation, manufacturing managers may similarly be reporting to people who rose through the ranks of engineering and finance.

We could handle the problem by designating one person the senior manufacturing manager and having all the manufacturing managers report to him instead of to the general manager. But the more we do this, the more we move toward a totally functional form of organization. A general manager could no longer coordinate the activities of the finance, marketing, engineering, and manufacturing groups toward a single business purpose responsive to marketplace needs. We want the immediacy and the operating priorities coming from the general manager as well as a technical supervisory relationship. The solution is dual reporting.

But does the technical supervisor's role have to be filled by a single individual? No. Consider the following scenario, which could be taken from an ordinary day at Intel. Our manufacturing manager is sitting in the cafeteria having a cup of coffee, and the manufacturing manager from another division (whose boss, the general manager, has a finance background) comes over. They start chatting about what's going on in their respective divisions and begin to realize that they have a number of technical problems in common. Applying the theory that two heads are better than one, they decide to meet a bit more often. Eventually the meetings become regularly scheduled and manufacturing managers from other divisions join the two to exchange views about problems they share. Pretty soon a committee or a council made up of a group of peers comes into existence to tackle issues common to all. In short, they have found a way to deal with those technical issues that their bosses, the general managers, can't help them with. In effect, they now have supervision that a general manager competent in manufacturing could have given them, but that supervision is being exercised by a *peer group*. The manufacturing managers report to two supervisors: to this group and to their respective general managers, as the figure opposite shows.

To make such a body work requires the *voluntary surrender of individual decision-making to the group*. Being a member means you no longer have complete freedom of individual action, because you must go along with the decisions of your peers in most instances. By analogy, think of yourself as one of a couple who decides to take a vacation with another couple. You know that if you go together you will not be free to do exactly what you want to do when you want to do it, but you go together anyway because you'll have more fun, even while you'll have less

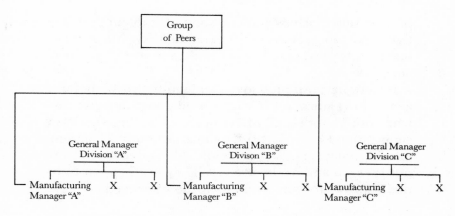

The manufacturing managers report to two supervisors: to their general managers and to a group of their peers.

freedom. At work, surrendering individual decision-making depends on trusting the soundness of actions taken by your group of peers.

Trust in no way relates to an organizational principle but is instead an aspect of the corporate culture, something about which much has been written in recent years. Put simply, it is a set of values and beliefs, as well as familiarity with the way things are done and should be done in a company. The point is that a strong and positive corporate culture is absolutely essential if dual reporting and decision-making by peers are to work.

This system makes a manager's life ambiguous, and most people don't like ambiguity. Nevertheless, the system is needed to make hybrid organizations work, and while people will strive to find something simpler, the reality is that it doesn't exist. A strictly functional organization, which is clear conceptually, tends to remove engineering and manufacturing (or the equivalent groups in your firm) from the marketplace, leaving them with no idea of what the customers want. A highly mission-oriented organization, in turn, may have definite crisp reporting relationships and clear and unambiguous objectives at all times. However, the fragmented state of affairs that results causes inefficiency and poor overall performance.

It's not because Intel loved ambiguity that we became a hybrid organization. We have tried everything else, and while other models may have been less ambiguous, they simply didn't work. Hybrid organizations and the accompanying dual reporting principle, like a democracy, are not great in and of themselves. They just happen to be the best way for any business to be organized.

Making Hybrid Organizations Work

To make hybrid organizations work, you need a way to coordinate the mission-oriented units and the functional groups so that the resources of the latter are allocated and delivered to meet the needs of the former. Consider how the controller works at Intel. His professional methods, practices, and standards are set by the functional group to which he belongs, the finance organization. Consequently, the controller for a business unit should report to someone in both the functional and the mission-oriented organizations, with the type of supervision reflecting the varying needs of the two. The divisional general manager gives the controller mission-oriented priorities by asking him to work on specific business problems. The finance manager makes sure that the controller is trained to do his work in a technically proficient manner, supervises and monitors his technical performance, and looks after his career inside finance, promoting him, perhaps, to the position of controller of a bigger, more complex division if he performs well. Again, as shown opposite, this is dual reporting, the management principle that enables the hybrid organization form to work.

The example has parallels throughout a corporation.

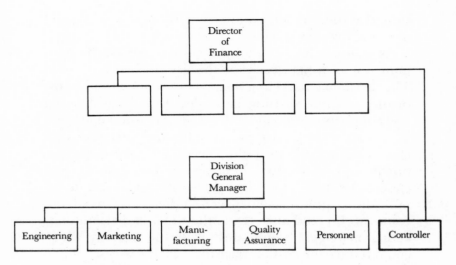

The controller for a business division should be supervised by both organizations.

Consider advertising. Should each business division devise and pursue its own advertising campaign, or should all of it be handled through a single corporate entity? As before, there are pros and cons on both sides. Each division clearly understands its own strategy best, and therefore presumably best understands what its advertising message should be and to whom it should be aimed. This would suggest that advertising stay in the hands of the divisions. On the other hand, the products of various divisions often all serve the needs of a specific market, and taken together represent a much more complete solution to the customers' needs than what can be provided by an individual division. Here the customer and hence the manufacturer clearly benefit if all the advertising stories are told in a coherent, coordinated fashion. Also, advertising sells not just a specific product but the entire corporation as well. Because the ads ought to project a consistent image that is right for everybody, we should at the very least not let a division go out and hire its own advertising agency.

As with much else in a hybrid organization, the optimum solution here calls for the use of dual reporting. The divisional marketing managers should control most of their own advertising messages. But a coordinating body of peers consisting of the various divisional marketing managers and perhaps chaired by the corporate merchandising manager should provide the necessary functional supervision for all involved. This body would choose the advertising agency, for instance, and determine the graphic image to which *all* divisional ads should conform. It could also define the way the division marketing managers would deal with the agency, which could reduce the cost of space through the use of volume buying. Yet the specific selling message communicated by an individual ad would be mainly left to the divisional people.

Dual reporting can certainly tax the patience of the marketing managers, as they are now also required to understand the needs and thought processes of their peers. But no real alternative exists when you need to communicate individual product and market messages and maintain a corporate identity at the same time.

We have seen that all kinds of organizations evolve into a hybrid organizational form. They must also develop a system of dual reporting. Consider the following story about Ohio University that appeared in the *Wall Street Journal* (bracketed comments are mine):

> A university is an odd place to manage. The president of the University said, "There's clearly a shared responsibility for decision-making between administration [functional organization] and faculty [mission-oriented organization]." A University Planning Advisory Council [a group of peers] was formed with representation from the faculty and administra-

tion to help allocate limited resources [a most difficult and common problem] in the face of severe budget cuts. "We are being educated to think institutionally," said one council member. "I'm representing student affairs, which had some projects up for consideration this year. But I made a big pitch for buying a new bulldozer."

So to put it yet another way, the hybrid organizational form is the inevitable consequence of enjoying the benefits of being part of a large organization—a company or university or whatever. To be sure, neither that form nor the need for dual reporting is an excuse for needless busywork, and we should mercilessly slash away unnecessary bureaucratic hindrance, apply work simplification to all we do, and continually subject all established requirements for coordination and consultation to the test of common sense. But we should not expect to escape from complexity by playing with reporting arrangements. Like it or not, the hybrid organization is a fundamental phenomenon of organizational life.

Another Wrinkle: The Two-Plane Organization

Whenever a person becomes involved in coordination—something not part of his regular daily work—we encounter a subtle variation of dual reporting.

Remember Cindy, the know-how manager responsible for maintaining and improving a specific manufacturing process? Cindy reports to a supervising engineer, who in turn reports to the engineering manager of the plant. In her daily work, Cindy keeps things going by manipulating the manufacturing equipment, watching the process monitors, and making adjustments when necessary. But Cindy has another job, too. She meets formally once a month with her counterparts from the other production plants to identify, discuss, and solve problems related to the process for which they are each responsible in their respective plants. This coordinating group also works to standardize procedures used at all plants. The work of Cindy's group, and others like it, is supervised by another more senior group (called the Engineering Managers Council), which is made up of the engineering managers from all the plants.

Cindy's various reporting relationships can be found in the figure below. As we can see, as a process engineer in the production plant, where she spends 80 percent of her time, Cindy has a clear, crisp reporting arrangement to her supervising engineer, and through him, to the

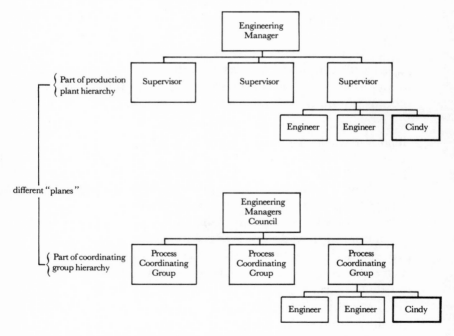

Cindy's name appears on two organization charts—coordinating groups are a means for know-how managers to increase their leverage.

plant engineering manager. But as a member of the process coordinating group, she is also supervised by its chairman. So we see that Cindy's name appears on two organization charts that serve two separate purposes—one to operate the production plant, the other to coordinate the efforts of various plants. Again we see dual reporting because Cindy has two supervisors.

Cindy's two responsibilities won't fit on a single organization chart. Instead, we have to think of the coordinating group as existing on a different chart, or on a different plane. This sounds complicated but really isn't. If Cindy belonged to a church, she would be regarded a member of that organization as well as being part of Intel. Her supervisor there, as it were, would be the local pastor, who in turn is a member of the church hierarchy. No one would confuse these two roles: clearly operating on different planes, each has its own hierarchies, and that Cindy is a member of both groups at the same time would hardly trouble anyone. Cindy's being part of a coordinating group is like her church membership.

Our ability to use Cindy's skill and know-how in two different capacities makes it possible for her to exert a much larger leverage at Intel. In her main job, her knowledge affects the work that takes place in one plant; in her second, through what she does in the process coordinating group, she can influence the work of *all* plants. So we see that the existence of such groups is a way for managers, especially know-how managers, to increase their leverage.

The two-plane concept is a part of everyday organizational life. For instance, while people mostly work at an operating task, they also plan. The hierarchy of the corporation's planning bodies lies on a plane separate from the one on which you'll find the operating groups. Moreover, if a person can operate in two planes, he can operate in three. Cindy could also be part of a task force to achieve a specific result in which her expertise is needed. This is as if Cindy were to work at Intel, to belong to a church, and to do advisory work for the town's parks department. These are separate roles and do not conflict with one another, though they all do vie for Cindy's time.

It could also turn out that people who are in a subordinate/supervisory relationship in one plane might find the relationship reversed in another. For example, I am president of Intel, but in another plane I am a member of a strategic planning group, where I report to its chairman, who is one of our division controllers. It's as if I were a member of the Army Reserve, and on our weekend exercises I found myself under the command of a regimental leader who happens to be this division controller. Back at the operating ranch, I may be his supervisor or his supervisor's supervisor, but in the Army Reserve he is my commanding officer.

The point is that the two- (or multi-) plane organization is very useful. Without it I could only participate if I were in charge of everything I was part of. I don't have that kind of time, and often I'm not the most qualified person around to lead. The multi-plane organization enables me to serve as a foot soldier rather than as a general when appropriate and useful. This gives the organization important flexibility.

Many of the groups that we are talking about here are temporary. Some, like task forces, are specifically formed for a purpose, while others are merely an informal collection of people who work together to solve a particular problem. Both cease to work as a group once the problem has been handled. The more varied the nature of the problems we face and the more rapidly things change around us, the more we have to rely on such specially composed *transitory teams* to cope with matters. In the electronics business, we can't possibly shift formal organization fast enough to keep up with the pace of advancing technology. The techniques that we have to master to make hybrid organizations work—dual or multiple reporting and also decision-making by peer groups—are both necessary if such transitory teams are to work. The key factor common to all is the use of cultural values as a mode of control, which we will consider next.

10

Modes of
Control

Let's look at the ways in which our actions can be controlled or influenced. Say you need new tires for your car. You go down the street to the dealer and take a look at the various lines he has to offer. Then you'll probably go up the street to see what the competition has. Maybe later you'll turn to a consumer magazine to help you choose. Eventually, you'll make a decision based on one thing: your own *self-interest*. You want to buy the tires you think will meet your needs at the lowest cost to you. It is quite unlikely that any personal feelings toward the tire dealer will come to mind. You are not concerned about *his* welfare—there's not much chance that you would say to him that he isn't charging you enough for the tires.

Now you have the tires on your car and you drive off. After a while, you come to a red light. You stop. Do you think about it? No. It's a law established by the society at large that everybody stops at a red light and you unquestioningly accept and live by it. Vehicular chaos would reign if all drivers had not entered into a *contract* to stop. The traffic cop monitors adherence and penalizes those who break the law.

After the light changes, you continue on down the road and come upon the scene of a major accident. Quite likely, you'll forget about laws like not stopping on a freeway and also forget about your own self-interest: you'll probably do everything you can to help the accident victims and, in the meantime, expose yourself to all kinds of dangers and risks. What motivates you now is not at all what did when you were shopping for tires or stopping at the red light: not self-interest or obeying the law, but concern about someone else's life.

Similarly, our behavior in a work environment can be controlled by three invisible and pervasive means. These are:

- free-market forces
- contractual obligations
- cultural values

Free-Market Forces

When you bought your tires, your actions were governed by free-market forces, which are based on price: goods and services are being exchanged between two entities (individuals, organizational units, or corporations), with each seeking only to enrich himself or itself. This is very simple. It is a matter of "I want to buy the tire at the lowest price I can get" versus "I want to sell the tire at the highest price I can get." Neither party here cares if the other goes bankrupt, nor do they pretend to. This is a very efficient way to buy and sell tires. No one is needed to oversee the transaction because everyone is openly serving his own self-interest.

So why aren't the forces of the marketplace used all the time in all circumstances? Because to work, the goods and services bought and sold must possess a very clearly defined dollar value. The free market can easily establish a price for something as simple as tires. But for much else that changes hands in a work or business environment, value is hard to establish.

Contractual Obligations

Transactions between companies are usually governed by the free market. When we buy a commodity product from a vendor, we are trying to get it at the best possible price, and vice versa. But what happens when the value of something is not easily defined? What happens, for instance, when it takes a *group* of people to accomplish a certain task? How much does each of them contribute to the value the business adds to the product? The point is that how much an engineer is worth in a group cannot be pinned down by appealing to the free market. In fact, if we bought engineering work by the "bit," I think we would end up spending more time trying to decide the value of each bit of contribution than the contribution itself is worth. Here trying to use free-market concepts becomes quite inefficient.

So you say to the engineers, "Okay, I'll retain your services for a year for a set amount of money, and you will agree to do a certain type of work in return. We've now entered into a contract. I'll give you an office and a terminal, and you promise me to do the best you can to perform your task."

The nature of control is now based on contractual obligations, which define the kind of work you will do and the standards that will govern it. Because I can't specify in advance exactly what you will do from day to day, I must have a fair amount of generalized authority over your work. So you must give to me as part of the contract the right to monitor and evaluate and, if necessary, correct your work. We agree on other guidelines and work out rules that we will both obey.

In return for stopping at a red light, we count on other drivers to do the same thing, and we can drive through green lights. But for lawbreakers we need policemen, and with them, as with supervisors, we introduce *overhead*.

What are some other examples of contractual obligation? Take the tax system. We surrender the right to
some of what we earn and expect certain services in
return. Giant overhead is necessary to monitor and audit
our tax returns. A utility company presents another example. Its representatives will go to somebody who
works for the government and say, "I'll build a three-
hundred-million-dollar generating plant and provide
electricity for this portion of the state if you promise me
that no one else will build one and try to sell electricity
here." The state says, "Well, that's fine, but we're not
going to let you charge whatever you want for the power
you generate. We'll establish a monitoring agency called
the Public Utilities Commission and they'll tell you how
much you can charge consumers and how much profit
you can make." So, in exchange for a monopoly, the
company is contractually obliged to accept the government's decision on pricing and profit.

Cultural Values

When the environment changes more rapidly than one
can change rules, or when a set of circumstances is so
ambiguous and unclear that a contract between the parties that attempted to cover all possibilities would be
prohibitively complicated, we need another mode of
control, which is based on cultural values. Its most important characteristic is that the interest of the larger
group to which an individual belongs takes precedence
over the interest of the individual himself. When such
values are at work, some emotionally loaded words come
into play—words like *trust*—because you are surrendering to the group your ability to protect yourself. And for
this to happen, you must believe that you all share a
common set of *values,* a common set of *objectives,* and a
common set of *methods.* These, in turn, can only be developed by a great deal of common, shared experience.

The Role of Management

You don't need management to supervise the workings of free-market forces; no one supervises sales made at a flea market. In a contractual obligation, management has a role in setting and modifying the rules, monitoring adherence to them, and evaluating and improving performance. As for cultural values, management has to develop and nurture the common set of values, objectives, and methods essential for the existence of trust. How do we do that? One way is by *articulation,* by spelling out these values, objectives, and methods. The other, even more important, way is by *example.* If our behavior at work will be regarded as in line with the values we profess, that fosters the development of a group culture.

The Most Appropriate Mode of Control

There is a temptation to idealize what I've called cultural values as a mode of control because it is so "nice," even utopian, because everybody presumably cares about the common good and subjugates self-interest to that common good. But this is not the most efficient mode of control under all conditions. It is no guide to buying tires, nor could the tax system work this way. Accordingly, given a certain set of conditions, there is always a *most appropriate* mode of control, which we as managers should find and use.

How do we do that? There are two variables here: first, the nature of a person's motivation; and second, the nature of the environment in which he works. An imaginary composite index can be applied to measure an environment's complexity, uncertainty, and ambiguity, which we'll call the *CUA factor.* Cindy, the process engineer, is surrounded by tricky technologies, new and not fully operational equipment, and development engineers and production engineers pulling her in opposite

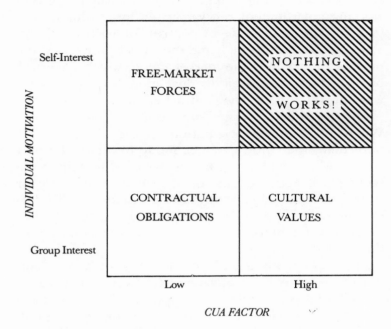

Self-Interest

INDIVIDUAL MOTIVATION

	FREE-MARKET FORCES	NOTHING WORKS!
	CONTRACTUAL OBLIGATIONS	CULTURAL VALUES

Group Interest

Low   High

CUA FACTOR

It is our task as managers to identify which mode of control is most appropriate.

directions. Her working environment, in short, is *complex.* Bruce, the marketing manager, has asked for permission to hire more people for his grossly understaffed group; his supervisor waffles, and Bruce is left with no idea if he'll get the go-ahead or what to do if he doesn't. Bruce's working environment is *uncertain.* Mike, whom we will now introduce as an Intel transportation supervisor, had to deal with so many committees, councils, and divisional manufacturing managers that he didn't know which, if any, end was up. He eventually quit, unable to tolerate the *ambiguity* of his working environment.

Let's now conceive a simple chart with four quadrants, shown above. The individual motivation can run from

self-interest to group-interest, and the CUA factor of a
working environment can vary from low to high. Now
look for the best mode of control for each quadrant.
When self-interest is high and the CUA factor is low, the
most appropriate is the market mode, which governed
our tire purchase. As individual motivation moves toward group interest, the contractual mode becomes appropriate, which governed our stopping for a red light.
When group-interest orientation and the CUA factor are
both high, the cultural values mode becomes the best
choice, which explains to us why we tried to help at the
scene of the accident. And finally, when the CUA factor
is high and individual motivation is based on self-interest, *no* mode of control will work well. This situation, like
√ every man for himself on a sinking ship, can only produce *chaos*.

Let's apply our model to the work of a new employee. What is his motivation? It is very much based
on self-interest. So you should give him a clearly structured job with a low CUA factor. If he does well, he will
begin to feel more at home, worry less about himself,
and start to care more about his team. He learns that if
he is on a boat and wants to get ahead, it is better for
him to help row than to run to the bow. The employee
can then be promoted into a more complex, uncertain,
ambiguous job. (These tend to pay more.) As time
passes, he will continue to gain an increasing amount
of shared experience with other members of the organization and will be ready to tackle more and more
complex, ambiguous, and uncertain tasks. This is why
promotion from within tends to be the approach favored by corporations with strong corporate cultures.
Bring young people in at relatively low-level, well-
defined jobs with low CUA factors, and over time they
will share experiences with their peers, supervisors, and
subordinates and will learn the values, objectives, and

methods of the organization. They will gradually accept, even flourish in, the complex world of multiple bosses and peer decision-making.

But what do we do when for some reason we have to hire a senior person from outside the company? Like any other new hire, he too will come in having high self-interest, but inevitably we will give him an organization to manage that is in trouble; after all, that was our reason for going outside. So not only does our new manager have a tough job facing him, but his working environment will have a very high CUA. Meanwhile, he has no base of common experience with the rest of the organization and no knowledge of the methods used to help him work. All we can do is cross our fingers and hope he quickly forgets self-interest and just as quickly gets on top of his job to reduce his CUA factor. Short of that, he's probably out of luck.

Modes of Control at Work

At any one time, one of the three modes of control may govern what we are doing. But from one day to the next, we find ourselves influenced by all three. Let's track Bob's mode of control for a bit. When Bob, a marketing supervisor, buys his lunch in the cafeteria, he's influenced by market forces. His choices are well defined and based on what he wants to buy and what he wants to pay. Bob's coming to work in the first place represents a transaction governed by contractual obligations. He is paid a set salary for doing his best, which implies that he has to show up. And his willingness to participate in strategic planning activities shows cultural values at work. This is work outside of his "regular" job as defined contractually, and so represents extra effort for him. But he does it because he feels the company needs what he has to contribute.

Let's now consider what goes on during the course of a work project. As we know, Barbara's department is responsible for training the Intel sales force in her division's products. When she buys materials used in the training program, free-market forces reign as binders of the required quality are purchased at the lowest possible price. The existence of the training program itself, however, presents an example of contractual obligations at work. The salespeople *expect* that each division will provide training on a regular basis. While the program isn't a mandated requirement spelled out somewhere in a formal policy statement, its basis is nonetheless contractual. The point is, expectations can be as binding as a legal document.

When a number of divisions share a common sales force, each of them has a vested interest to train representatives to promote and sell its products. At the same time, unless the divisions are willing to sacrifice self-interest in favor of the common interest, the training sessions can easily become disjointed free-for-alls and confuse everybody. So the need to have the individual divisions present coordinated messages is governed by corporate values. Thus, in field sales training, we find all three modes of control at work.

Recently a group of factory marketing managers claimed that our salespeople were governed only by self-interest. They said that they devoted most of their attention to selling those items that produced the most commissions and bonuses. Irritated and a bit self-righteous, the managers felt they were much more concerned about the common good of the company than were their colleagues in the field.

But the marketing departments themselves created the monster. To get the sales force to favor particular products, the divisions had for some time been running contests, with prizes ranging from cash bonuses to trips to exotic places. The marketing managers were compet-

ing against one another for a finite and valuable resource: the salesmen's time. And the salesmen merely
responded as one might expect.

But salespeople can also behave in the opposite fashion. At one time, one of our divisions had serious problems, leaving the sales engineers with no product to sell
for nearly a year. They could have left Intel and immediately gotten other jobs and quick commissions elsewhere, but by and large they stayed with us. They stayed
because they believed in the company and had faith that
eventually things would get better. Belief and faith are
not aspects of the market mode, but stem from adherence to cultural values.

Part Four
THE
PLAYERS

11

The Sports
Analogy

Earlier I built a case summed up by the key sentence: A
manager's output is the output of the organization under
his supervision or influence.

Put another way, this means that management is a
team activity. But no matter how well a team is put together, no matter how well it is directed, the team will
perform only as well as the individuals on it. In other
words, everything we've considered so far is useless unless the members of our team will continually try to offer
the best they can do. The means a manager has at his
disposal to elicit peak individual performance are what
the rest of this book is about.

When a person is not doing his job, there can only be
two reasons for it. The person either can't do it or won't
do it; he is either not capable or not motivated. To determine which, we can employ a simple mental test: if the
person's life depended on doing the work, could he do
it? If the answer is yes, that person is not motivated; if
the answer is no, he is not capable. If my life depended
on playing the violin on command, I could not do it. But
if I had to run a mile in six minutes, I probably could. Not
that I would want to, but if my life depended on it, I
probably could.

The single most important task of a manager is to elicit peak performance from his subordinates. So if two things limit high output, a manager has two ways to tackle the issue: through *training* and *motivation.* Each, as we see in the next figure, can improve a person's performance. In this chapter, our concern is motivation.

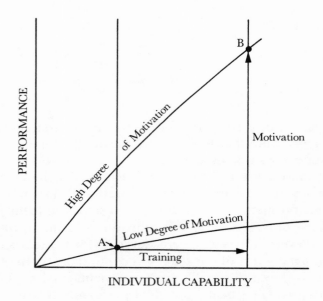

A manager has two ways to improve performance: training and motivation.

How does a manager motivate his subordinates? For most of us, the word implies doing something to another person. But I don't think that can happen, because motivation has to come from within somebody. Accordingly, all a manager can do is create an environment in which motivated people can flourish.

Because better motivation means better performance, not a change of attitude or feeling, a subordinate's saying "I feel motivated" means nothing. What matters is if he *performs* better or worse because his environment changed. An attitude may constitute an indicator, a "window into the black box" of human motivation, but it is not the desired result or output. Better performance at a given skill level is.

For most of Western history, including the early days of the Industrial Revolution, motivation was based mostly on fear of punishment. In Dickens' time, the threat of loss of life got people to work, because if people did not work, they were not paid and could not buy food, and if they stole food and got caught, they were hanged. The fear of punishment indirectly caused them to produce more than they might have otherwise.

Over the past thirty years or so, a number of new approaches have begun to replace older practices keyed to fear. Perhaps the emergence of the new, humanistic approaches to motivation can be traced to the decline in the relative importance of manual labor and the corresponding rise in the importance of so-called knowledge workers. The output of a manual laborer is readily measurable, and departures from the expected can be spotted and dealt with immediately. But for a knowledge worker, such departures take longer to determine because even the expectations themselves are very difficult to state precisely. In other words, fear won't work as well with computer architects as with galley slaves; hence, new approaches to motivation are needed.

My description of what makes people perform relies heavily on Abraham Maslow's theory of motivation, simply because my own observations of working life confirm Maslow's concepts. For Maslow, motivation is closely tied to the idea of *needs*, which cause people to have *drives*, which in turn result in *motivation*. A need once satisfied stops being a need and therefore stops being a source of motivation. Simply put, if we are to create and maintain a high degree of motivation, we must keep some needs unsatisfied at all times.

People, of course, tend to have a variety of concurrent needs, but one among them is always stronger than the others. And that need is the one that largely determines an individual's motivation and therefore his level of performance. Maslow defined a set of needs, as shown below, that tend to lie in a hierarchy: when a lower need is satisfied, one higher is likely to take over.

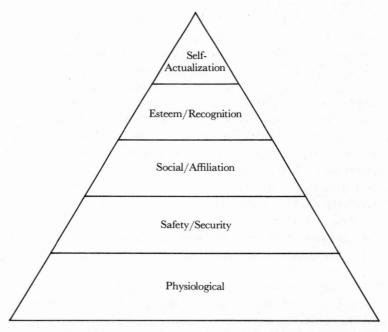

Maslow defined a set of needs that tend to lie in a hierarchy: when a lower need is satisfied, one higher is likely to take over.

Physiological Needs

These needs consist of things that money can buy, like food, clothing, and other basic necessities of life. Fear is hitched to such needs: one fears the possible deprivation of food, clothing, and so on.

Security/Safety Needs

These come from a desire to protect oneself from slipping back to a state of being deprived of the basic necessities. Safety and security needs are fulfilled, for example, when medical insurance provides employees protection against the fear of going bankrupt trying to pay doctor and hospital fees. The existence of benefits is rarely a dominant source of employee motivation, but if benefits were absent and employees had to worry about such concerns, performance would no doubt be badly affected.

Social/Affiliation Needs

The social needs stem from the inherent desire of human beings to belong to some group or other. But people don't want to belong to just any group; they need to belong to one whose members possess something in common with themselves. For example, when people are excited, confident, or happy, they want to be around people who are also excited, confident, or happy. Conversely, misery loves not just any company, but the company of other miserable people. Nobody who is miserable wants to be around someone happy.

Social needs are quite powerful. A friend of mine decided to go back to work after many years of minding her home. She took a low-paying job, which did little for her family's standard of living. For a long time, I didn't understand why she did what she did, but finally it dawned on me: she needed the companionship her work offered. Going to work meant being around a group of people she liked.

Another example of the power of social needs is provided by Jim, a young engineer. His first job after he graduated from college was with a very large, long-established company, while his two college roommates came to work at Intel. Because Jim continued to room with them, he was exposed to what working within Intel was like. Moreover, most of his roommates' friends from work were also young, unmarried, and just a year or two out of college, while most of the people where Jim worked were married and at least ten years older. Jim felt left out, and his need for a group in which he felt comfortable prompted him to come to work at Intel, though he very much enjoyed his work at the other company.

As one's environment or condition in life changes, one's desire to satisfy a particular set of needs is replaced by a desire to satisfy another set. There's the story of a young Intel manager, Chuck, when he was a first-year student at the Harvard Business School. Initially, he was engulfed by a fear of the class material, of his professors, of failure, of flunking out. After a while his fear gave way to the realization that everyone else was in the same boat, also afraid. Students began to form study groups whose ostensible purpose was to consider class material together, but whose real purpose was to strengthen confidence. Chuck moved from being governed largely by his need for sheer survival—a "physiological" need—to one for security and safety. As time went on, the study groups dissolved and the students started to associate with other members of the class. The entire class, or "section," as it was called, developed a definite and recognizable set of characteristics; it became, in short, a team. Members enjoyed belonging, associating, and identifying with it, and worked to sustain the section's image among the professors and other students. Chuck was now satisfying his need for affiliation.

Of course, regressive movement is also possible. Recently, a highly motivated, smoothly working team of manufacturing employees in one of our California plants was suddenly jolted—all too literally—from satisfying a very high level of human needs to abandoning an inventory of silicon wafers, expensive manufacturing equipment, even friends. An earthquake shook their factory. People feared for their lives, dropped everything, and ran to the nearest exit as they found themselves totally consumed by the most fundamental of all physiological needs—survival.

The physiological, safety/security, and social needs all can motivate us to show up for work, but other needs—esteem and self-actualization—make us perform once we are there.

Esteem/Recognition Needs

The need for esteem or recognition is readily apparent in the cliché "keeping up with the Joneses." Such striving is commonly frowned upon, but if an athlete's "Jones" is last year's Olympic gold medalist, or if an actor's "Jones" is Laurence Olivier, the need to keep up with or emulate someone is a powerful source of positive motivation. The person or group whose recognition you desire may mean nothing to someone else—esteem exists in the eyes of the beholder. If you are an aspiring high school athlete and one of the top players passes you in the hall and says hello, you'll feel terrific. Yet if you try to tell your family or friends how pleased you were about the encounter, you are likely to be met with blank stares, because the "hello" means nothing to people who are not aspiring athletes in your high school.

All of the sources of motivation we've talked about so far are self-limiting. That is, when a need is gratified, it can no longer motivate a person. Once a predetermined goal or level of achievement is reached, the need to go any further loses urgency. A friend of mine was thrust into a premature "mid-life crisis" when, in recognition of the excellent work he had been doing, he was named a vice president of the corporation. Such a position had been a life-long goal. When he had suddenly attained it, he found himself looking for some other way to motivate himself.

Self-Actualization Needs

For Maslow, self-actualization stems from a personal realization that "what I can be, I must be." The title of a movie about athletes, *Personal Best,* captures what self-actualization means: the need to achieve one's utter personal best in a chosen field of endeavor. Once someone's source of motivation is self-actualization, his drive to perform has no limit. Thus, its most important characteristic is that unlike other sources of motivation, which extinguish themselves after the needs are fulfilled, self-actualization continues to motivate people to ever higher levels of performance.

Two inner forces can drive a person to use all of his capabilities. He can be *competence*-driven or *achievement*-driven. The former concerns itself with job or task mastery. A virtuoso violinist who continues to practice day after day is obviously moved by something other than a need for esteem and recognition. He works to sharpen his own skill, trying to do a little bit better this time than the time before, just as a teenager on a skateboard practices the same trick over and over again. The same teenager may not sit still for ten minutes to do homework, but on a skateboard he is relentless, driven by the self-actualization need, a need to get better that has no limit.

The achievement-driven path to self-actualization is not quite like this. Some people—*not* the majority—are moved by an abstract need to achieve in all that they do. A psychology lab experiment illustrated the behavior of such people. Some volunteers were put into a room in which pegs were set at various places on the floor. Each person was given some rings but not instructed what to do with them. People eventually started to toss the rings onto the pegs. Some casually tossed the rings at faraway pegs; others stood over the pegs and dropped the rings down onto them. Still others walked just far enough away from the pegs so that to toss a ring onto a peg constituted a challenge. These people worked at the boundary of their capability.

Researchers classified the three types of behavior. The first group, termed gamblers, took high risks but exerted no influence on the outcome of events. The second group, termed conservatives, were people who took very little risk. The third group, termed achievers, had to test the limits of what they could do, and with no prompting demonstrated the point of the experiment: namely, that some people simply *must* test themselves. By challenging themselves, these people were likely to miss a peg several times, but when they began to ring the peg consistently, they gained satisfaction and a sense of achievement. The point is that both competence- and achievement-oriented people *spontaneously* try to test the outer limits of their abilities.

When the need to stretch is not spontaneous, management needs to create an environment to foster it. In an MBO system, for example, objectives should be set at a point high enough so that even if the individual (or organization) pushes himself hard, he will still only have a fifty-fifty chance of making them. Output will tend to be greater when everybody strives for a level of achievement beyond his immediate grasp, even though trying means failure half the time. Such goal-setting is extremely important if what you want is peak performance from yourself and your subordinates.

Moreover, if we want to cultivate achievement-driven motivation, we need to create an environment that values and emphasizes *output.* My first job was with a research and development laboratory, where a lot of people were very highly motivated but tended to be knowledge-centered. They were driven to know more, but not necessarily to know more in order to produce concrete results. Consequently, relatively little was actually *achieved*. The value system at Intel is completely the reverse. The Ph.D. in computer science who knows an answer in the abstract, yet does not apply it to create some tangible output, gets little recognition, but a junior engineer who produces results is highly valued and esteemed. And that is how it should be.

Money and Task-Relevant Feedback

We now come to the question of how money motivates people. At the lower levels of the motivation hierarchy, money is obviously important, needed to buy the necessities of life. Once there is enough money to bring a person up to a level he expects of himself, more money will not motivate. Consider people who work at our assembly plant in the Caribbean. The standard of living there is quite low, and people who work for us enjoy one substantially higher than most of the population. Yet, in the early years of operation, many employees worked just long enough to accumulate some small sum of money and then quit. For them, money's motivation was clearly limited; having reached a predetermined notion of how much money they wanted, more money and a steady job provided no more motivation.

Now consider a venture capitalist who after making ten million dollars is still very hard at work trying to make another ten. Physiological, safety, or social needs hardly apply here. Moreover, because venture capitalists usually don't publicize their successes, they are not driven by a need for esteem or recognition. So it appears that at the upper level of the need hierarchy, when one is self-actualized, money in itself is no longer a source of motivation but rather a *measure of achievement*. Money in the physiological- and security-driven modes only motivates until the need is satisfied, but money as a measure ✓ of achievement will motivate without limit. Thus the second ten million can be just as important to the venture capitalist as the first, since it is not the utilitarian need for the money that drives him but the achievement that it implies, and the need for achievement is boundless.

A simple test can be used to determine where someone is in the motivational hierarchy. If the absolute sum of a raise in salary an individual receives is important to him, he is working mostly within the physiological or safety modes. If, however, what matters to him is how his raise stacks up against what other people got, he is motivated by esteem/recognition or self-actualization, because in this case money is clearly a *measure*.

Once in the self-actualization mode, a person needs measures to gauge his progress and achievement. The most important type of measure is feedback on his performance. For the self-actualized person driven to improve his competence, the feedback mechanism lies within that individual himself. Our virtuoso violinist knows how the music should sound, knows when it is not right, and will strive tirelessly to get it right. Accordingly, if the possibility for improvement does not exist, the desire to keep practicing vanishes. I knew an Olympic fencing champion, a Hungarian who immigrated to this country. When I ran into him recently, he told me that he had quit fencing shortly after arriving in the U.S. He said that the level of competition here was not high enough to produce someone who could give him a contest, and that he couldn't bear to fence any longer because every time he did, he felt his skill was diminishing.

What are some of the feedback mechanisms or measures in the workplace? The most appropriate measures tie an employee's performance to the workings of the organization. If performance indicators and milestones in a management-by-objectives system are linked to the performance of the individual, they will gauge his degree of success and will enhance his progress. An obvious and very important responsibility of a manager is to steer his people away from irrelevant and meaningless rewards, such as office size or decor, and toward relevant and significant ones. The most important form of such *task-relevant feedback* is the performance review every subordinate should receive from his supervisor. More about this later.

Fear

In physiological and security/safety need–dominated motivation, one fears the loss of life or limb or loss of job or liberty. Does fear have a place in the esteem or self-actualized modes? It does, but here it becomes the *fear of failure*. But is that a positive or negative source of motivation? It can be either. Given a specific task, fear of failure can spur a person on, but if it becomes a preoccupation, a person driven by a need to achieve will simply become conservative. Let's think back to the ring tossers. If a person got an electrical shock each time he threw a ring and missed, soon enough he would walk over to the peg and drop the ring from directly over it to eliminate the pain associated with failure.

In general, in the upper levels of motivation, fear is not something coming from the outside. It is instead fear of not satisfying yourself that causes you to back off. You cannot stay in the self-actualized mode if you're always worried about failure.

The Sports Analogy

We've studied motivation to try to understand what makes people want to work so that as managers we can elicit peak performance from our subordinates—their "personal best." Of course, what we are really after is the performance of the organization as a whole, but that depends on how skilled and motivated the people within it are. Thus, our role as managers is, first, to train the individuals (to move them along the horizontal axis shown in the illustration on page 158), and, second, to bring them to the point where self-actualization motivates them, because once there, their motivation will be self-sustaining and limitless.

Is there a systematic way to lead people to self-actualization? For an answer, let's ask another question. Why does a person who is not terribly interested in his work at the office stretch himself to the limit running a marathon? What makes him run? *He is trying to beat other people or the stopwatch.* This is a simple model of self-actualization, wherein people will exert themselves to previously undreamed heights, forcing themselves to run farther or faster, while their efforts fill barrels with sweat. They will do this not for money, but just to beat the distance, the clock, or other people. Consider what made Joe Frazier box:

> It astounds Joe Frazier that anyone has to ask why he fights. "This is what I do. I am a fighter," he says. "It's my job. I'm just doing my job." Joe doesn't deny the attractiveness of money. "Who wants to work for nothing?" But there are things more important than money. "I don't need to be a star, because I don't need to shine. But I do need to be a boxer, because that's what I am. It's as simple as that."

Imagine how productive our country would become if managers could endow all work with the characteristics of competitive sports.

To try to do this, we must first overcome cultural prejudice. Our society respects someone's throwing himself into sports, but anybody who works very long hours is regarded as sick, a *workaholic.* So the prejudices of the majority say that sports are good and fun, but work is drudgery, a necessary evil, and in no way a source of pleasure.

That makes the cliché apply: if you can't beat them, join them—endow work with the characteristics of competitive sports. And the best way to get that spirit into the workplace is to establish some rules of the game and ways for employees to measure themselves. Eliciting peak performance means going up against something or somebody. Let me give you a simple example. For years the performance of the Intel facilities maintenance group, which is responsible for keeping our buildings clean and neat, was mediocre, and no amount of pressure or inducement seemed to do any good. We then initiated a program in which each building's upkeep was periodically scored by a resident senior manager, dubbed a "building czar." The score was then compared with those given the other buildings. The condition of *all of them* dramatically improved almost immediately. Nothing else was done; people did not get more money or other rewards. What they did get was a racetrack, an arena of competition. If your work is facilities maintenance, having your building receive the top score is a powerful source of motivation. This is key to the manager's approach and involvement: he has to see the work as it is seen by the people who do that work every day and then create indicators so that his subordinates can watch their "racetrack" take shape.

Conversely, of course, when the competition is removed, motivation associated with it vanishes. Consider the example of a newspaper columnist reflecting on his past. This journalist "thrived on beating the competition in the column, and his pleasure in his work began to wane after [his paper and the competitive paper] merged. 'I'll never forget that day of the merger,' the columnist said. 'I walked out to get the train, and I just thought: There isn't anyone else to beat.' "

Comparing our work to sports may also teach us how to cope with failure. As noted, one of the big impediments to a fully committed, highly motivated state of mind is preoccupation with failure. Yet we know that in any competitive sport, at least 50 percent of all matches are lost. All participants know that from the outset, and yet rarely do they give up at any stage of a contest.

The role of the manager here is also clear: it is that of the *coach*. First, an ideal coach takes no personal credit for the success of his team, and because of that his players trust him. Second, he is tough on his team. By being critical, he tries to get the best performance his team members can provide. Third, a good coach was likely a good player himself at one time. And having played the game well, he also understands it well.

Turning the workplace into a playing field can turn our subordinates into "athletes" dedicated to performing at the limit of their capabilities—the key to making our team consistent winners.

12

Task-Relevant
Maturity

I'll say again that a manager's most important responsibility is to elicit top performance from his subordinates. Assuming we understand what motivates an employee, the question becomes: Is there a single best management style, one approach that will work better than all others?

Many have looked for that optimum. Considering the issue historically, the management style most in favor seems to have changed to parallel the theory of motivation espoused at the time. At the turn of the century, ideas about work were simple. People were told what to do, and if they did it, they were paid; if they did not, they were fired. The corresponding leadership style was crisp and hierarchical: there were those who gave orders and those who took orders and executed them without question. In the 1950's, management theory shifted toward a humanistic set of beliefs that held that there was a nicer way to get people to work. The favored leadership style changed accordingly. Finally, as university behavioral science departments developed and grew, the theories of motivation and leadership became subjects of carefully controlled experiments. Surprisingly, none of the early intuitive presumptions could be borne out: the hard findings simply would not show that one style of leadership was better than another. It was hard to escape the conclusion that no optimal management style existed.

My own observations bear this out. At Intel we frequently rotate middle managers from one group to another in order to broaden their experience. These groups tend to be similar in background and in the type of work that they do, although their output tends to vary greatly. Some managers and their groups demonstrate themselves to be higher producers; others do not. The result of moving the managers about is often surprising. Neither the managers nor the groups maintain the characteristic of being either high-producing or low-producing as the managers are switched around. The inevitable conclusion is that high output is associated with particular *combinations* of certain managers and certain groups of workers. This also suggests that a given managerial approach is not equally effective under all conditions.

Some researchers in this field argue that there is a fundamental variable that tells you what the best management style is in a particular situation. That variable is the task-relevant maturity (TRM) of the subordinates, which is a combination of the degree of their achievement orientation and readiness to take responsibility, as well as their education, training, and experience. Moreover, all this is very specific to the task at hand, and it is entirely possible for a person or a group of people to have a TRM that is high in one job but low in another.

Let me give you an example of what I mean. We recently moved an extremely productive sales manager from the field into the plant, where he was placed in charge of a factory unit. The size and scope of the two jobs were comparable, yet the performance of the seasoned manager deteriorated, and he started to show the signs of someone overwhelmed by his work. What happened was that while the personal maturity of the manager obviously did not change, his task-relevant maturity in the new job was extremely low, since its environment, content, and tasks were all new to him. In time he learned to cope, and his TRM gradually increased. With that, his performance began to approach the outstanding levels he had exhibited earlier, which was why we promoted him in the first place. What happened here should have been totally predictable, yet we were surprised: we confused the manager's general competence and maturity with his task-relevant maturity.

Similarly, a person's TRM can be very high given a certain level of complexity, uncertainty, and ambiguity, but if the pace of the job accelerates or if the job itself abruptly changes, the TRM of that individual will drop. It's a bit like a person with many years' experience driving on small country roads being suddenly asked to drive on a crowded metropolitan freeway. His TRM driving his own car will drop precipitously.

The conclusion is that varying management styles are needed as task-relevant maturity varies. Specifically, when the TRM is low, the most effective approach is one that offers very precise and detailed instructions, wherein the supervisor tells the subordinate what needs to be done, when, and how: in other words, a highly structured approach. As the TRM of the subordinate grows, the most effective style moves from the structured to one more given to communication, emotional support, and encouragement, in which the manager pays more attention to the subordinate as an individual than to the task at hand. As the TRM becomes even greater, the effective management style changes again. Here the manager's involvement should be kept to a minimum, and should primarily consist of making sure that the objectives toward which the subordinate is working are mutually agreed upon. But regardless of what the TRM may be, the manager should always monitor a subordinate's work closely enough to avoid surprises. The presence or absence of monitoring, as we've said before, is the difference between a supervisor's *delegating* a task and *abdicating* it. The characteristics of the effective management style for the supervisor given the varying degrees of TRM are summarized in the table below.

A word of caution is in order: do not make a value judgment and consider a structured management style less worthy than a communication-oriented one. What is "nice" or "not nice" should have no place in how you think or what you do. Remember, we are after what is most *effective*.

The theory here parallels the development of the relationship between a parent and child. As the child matures, the most effective parental style changes, varying with the "life-relevant maturity"—or age—of the child. A parent needs to tell a toddler not to touch things that he might break or that might hurt him. The child cannot understand that the vase he wants to play with is an irreplaceable heirloom, but he can understand "no." As he grows older, he begins to do things on his own initiative, something the parent wants to encourage while still

TASK-RELEVANT MATURITY OF SUBORDINATE	CHARACTERISTICS OF THE EFFECTIVE MANAGEMENT STYLE
low	Structured; task-oriented; tell "what," "when," "how"
medium	Individual-oriented; emphasis on two-way communication, support, mutual reasoning
high	Involvement by manager minimal: establishing objectives and monitoring

The fundamental variable that determines the effective management style is the task-relevant maturity of the subordinate.

trying to keep him from injuring himself. A parent might suggest, for example, that his child give up his tricycle for his first two-wheeler. The parent will not simply send him out on his own, but will accompany him to keep the bicycle from tipping over while talking to him about safety on the streets. As the child's maturity continues to grow, the parent can cut back on specific instruction. When the child goes out to ride his bicycle, the parent no longer has to recite the litany of safety rules. Finally, when the life-relevant maturity of the child is high enough, he leaves home and perhaps goes away to college. At this point the relationship between parent and child will change again as the parent merely monitors the child's progress.

Should the child's environment suddenly change to one where his life-relevant maturity is inadequate (for example, if he runs into severe academic trouble), the parent may have to revert to a style used earlier.

As parental (or managerial) supervision moves from structured to communicating to monitoring, the degree of structure governing the behavior of the child (or the subordinate) does not really change. A teenager *knows* it is not safe to cross a busy interstate highway on his bicycle, and the parent no longer has to tell him not to do it. Structure moves from being *externally imposed* to being *internally given.*

If the parent (or supervisor) imparted early on to the child (or subordinate) the right way to do things (the correct operational values), later the child would be likely to make decisions the way the parent would. In fact, commonality of operational values, priorities, and preferences—how an organization works together—is a must if the progression in managerial style is to occur.

Without that commonality, an organization can become easily confused and lose its sense of purpose. Accordingly, the responsibility for transmitting common values rests squarely with the supervisor. He is, after all, accountable for the output of the people who report to him; then, too, without a shared set of values a supervisor cannot effectively delegate. An associate of mine who had always done an outstanding job hired a junior person to handle some old tasks, while he himself took on some new ones. The subordinate did poor work. My associate's reaction: "He has to make his own mistakes. That's how he learns!" The problem with this is that the subordinate's tuition is paid by his customers. And that is absolutely wrong. The responsibility for teaching the subordinate must be assumed by his supervisor, and not paid for by the customers of his organization, internal or external.

Management Style and Managerial Leverage

As supervisors, we should try to raise the task-relevant maturity of our subordinates as rapidly as possible for obvious pragmatic reasons. The appropriate management style for an employee with high TRM takes less time than detailed, structured, supervision requires. Moreover, once operational values are learned and TRM is high enough, the supervisor can delegate tasks to the subordinate, thus increasing his *managerial leverage*. Finally, at the highest levels of TRM, the subordinate's training is presumably complete, and motivation is likely to come from within, from self-actualization, which is the most powerful source of energy and effort a manager can harness.

As we've learned, a person's TRM depends on a specific working environment. When that changes, so will his TRM, as will his supervisor's most effective management style. Let's consider an army encampment where nothing ever happens. The sergeant in command has come to know each of his soldiers very well, and by and large maintains an informal relationship with them. The routines are so well established that he rarely has to tell anyone what to do; appropriate to the high TRM of the group, the sergeant contents himself with merely monitoring their activity. One day a jeepload of the enemy suddenly appears, coming over the hill and shooting at the camp. Instantly the sergeant reverts to a structured, task-oriented leadership style, barking orders at everyone, telling each of his soldiers what to do, when, and how. . . . After a while, if these skirmishes continue and the group keeps on fighting from the same place for a couple of months, this too will eventually become routine. With that, the TRM of the group for the new task —fighting—will increase. The sergeant can then gradually ease off telling everybody what to do.

Put another way, a manager's ability to operate in a style based on communication and mutual understanding depends on there being enough time for it. Though monitoring is on paper a manager's most productive approach, we have to work our way up to it in the real world. Even if we achieve it, if things suddenly change we have to revert quickly to the what-when-how mode.

That mode is one that we don't think an enlightened manager should use. As a result, we often don't take it up until it is too late and events overwhelm us. We managers must learn to fight such prejudices and regard any management mode not as either good or bad but rather as effective or not effective, given the TRM of our subordinates within a specific working environment. This is why researchers cannot find the single best way for a manager to work. It changes day by day and sometimes hour by hour.

It's Not Easy to Be a Good Manager

Deciding the TRM of your subordinates is not easy. Moreover, even if a manager knows what the TRM is, his personal preferences tend to override the logical and proper choice of management style. For instance, even if a manager sees that his subordinate's TRM is "medium" (see the table on page 175), in the real world the manager will likely opt for either the "structured" or "minimal" style. In other words, we want either to be fully immersed in the work of our subordinates, making their decisions, or to leave them completely alone, not wanting to be bothered.

Another problem here is a manager's perception of himself. We tend to see ourselves more as communicators and delegators than we really are, certainly much more than do our subordinates. I tested this conclusion by asking a group of managers to assess the management style of their supervisors, and then by asking those supervisors what they thought their style was. Some 90 percent of the supervisors saw their style as more communicating or delegating than their subordinates' view. What accounts for the large discrepancy? It is partly because managers think of themselves as perfect delegators. But also, sometimes a manager throws out suggestions to a subordinate who receives them as marching orders—furthering the difference in perceptions.

A manager once told me that his supervisor definitely practiced an effective communicating style with him because they skied and drank together. He was wrong. There is a huge distinction between a social relationship and a communicating *management* style, which is a caring involvement in the *work* of the subordinate. Close relationships off the job may help to create an equivalent relationship on the job, but they should not be confused. Two people I knew had a supervisor-subordinate relationship. They spent one week each year by themselves, fishing in a remote area. When fishing, they never talked about work—it being tacitly understood that work was off conversational limits. Oddly enough, their work relationship remained distant, their personal friendship having no effect on it.

This brings us to the age-old question of whether

friendship between supervisor and subordinate is a good thing. Some managers unhesitatingly assert that they never permit social relationships to develop with people they work with. In fact, there are pluses and minuses here. If the subordinate is a personal friend, the supervisor can move into a communicating management style quite easily, but the what-when-how mode becomes harder to revert to when necessary. It's unpleasant to give orders to a friend. I've seen several instances where a supervisor had to make a subordinate-friend toe a disciplinary line. In one case, a friendship was destroyed; in another, the supervisor's action worked out because the subordinate felt, thanks to the strength of the social relationship, that the supervisor was looking out for his (the subordinate's) professional interests.

Everyone must decide for himself what is professional and appropriate here. A test might be to imagine yourself delivering a tough performance review to your friend. Do you cringe at the thought? If so, don't make friends at work. If your stomach remains unaffected, you are likely to be someone whose personal relationships will strengthen work relationships.

13

Performance Appraisal: Manager as Judge and Jury

Why Bother?

Why are performance reviews a part of the management system of most organizations? And why do we review the performance of our subordinates? I posed both questions to a group of middle managers and got the following responses:

to assess the subordinate's work
to improve performance
to motivate
to provide feedback to a subordinate
to justify raises
to reward performance
to provide discipline
to provide work direction
to reinforce the company culture

Next, I asked the group to imagine themselves to be a supervisor giving a review to a subordinate, and asked them what their feelings were. Some of the answers:

pride
anger
anxiety

discomfort
guilt
empathy/concern
embarrassment
frustration

Finally, I asked the same group to think back to some
of the performance reviews they had received and asked
what, if anything, was wrong with them. Their answers
were quick and many:

review comments too general
mixed messages (inconsistent with rating or dollar
    raise)
no indication of how to improve
negatives avoided
supervisor didn't know my work
only recent performance considered
surprises

This should tell you that giving performance reviews
is a very complicated and difficult business and that we,
managers, don't do an especially good job at it.

The fact is that giving such reviews is the *single most
important form of task-relevant feedback* we as supervisors can
provide. It is how we assess our subordinates' level of
performance and how we deliver that assessment to them
individually. It is also how we allocate the rewards—
promotions, dollars, stock options, or whatever we may
use. As we saw earlier, the review will influence a subordinate's performance—positively or negatively—for a long
time, which makes the appraisal one of the manager's
highest-leverage activities. In short, the review is an extremely powerful mechanism, and it is little wonder that
opinions and feelings about it are strong and diverse.

But what is its fundamental purpose? Though all of
the responses given to my questions are correct, there is
one that is more important than any of the others: it is

to improve the subordinate's performance. The review is usually dedicated to two things: first, the *skill level* of the subordinate, to determine what skills are missing and to find ways to remedy that lack; and second, to intensify the subordinate's *motivation* in order to get him on a higher performance curve for the same skill level (see the illustration on page 158).

The review process also represents the most formal type of institutionalized leadership. It is the only time a manager is mandated to act as judge and jury: we managers are required by the organization that employs us to make a judgment regarding a fellow worker and then to deliver that judgment to him, face to face.

A supervisor's responsibility here is obviously very significant. What preparation have we had to do the job properly? About the only thing I can think of is that as subordinates we've been on the receiving end. But in general our society values avoiding confrontation. Even the word "argument" is frowned upon, something I learned many years ago when I first came to this country from Hungary. In Hungarian, the word "argument" is frequently used to describe a difference of opinion. When I began to learn English and used the word "argument," I would be corrected, as people would say, "Oh no, you don't mean 'argument,' you mean 'debate,' " or "you mean 'discussion.' " Among friends and peers you are not supposed to discuss politics, religion, or anything that might possibly produce a difference of opinion and a conflict. Football scores, gardening, and the weather are okay. We are taught that the well-mannered skirt potentially emotional issues. The point is, delivering a good performance review is really a unique act given both our cultural background and our professional training.

Don't think for a moment that performance reviews should be confined to large organizations. They should be part of managerial practice in organizations of any size and kind, from the insurance agent with two office assistants to administrators in education, government, and nonprofit organizations. The long and short of it: if performance matters in your operation, performance reviews are absolutely necessary.

Two aspects of the review—assessing performance and delivering the assessment—are equally difficult. Let's look at each in a little more detail.

Assessing Performance

Determining the performance of professional employees in a strictly objective manner is very difficult because there is obviously no cut-and-dried way to measure and characterize a professional employee's work completely. Most jobs involve activities that are not reflected by output in the time period covered by the review. Yet we have to give such activities appropriate weight as we assess a person's performance, even though we know we won't necessarily be objective, since only output can be measured with true objectivity. Anybody who supervises professionals, therefore, walks a tightrope: he needs to be objective, but must not be afraid of using his judgment, even though judgment is by definition subjective.

To make an assessment less difficult, a supervisor should clarify in his own mind in advance what it is that he expects from a subordinate and then attempt to judge whether he performed to expectations. The biggest problem with most reviews is that we don't usually define what it is we want from our subordinates, and, as noted earlier, if we don't know what we want, we are surely not going to get it.

Let's think back to our concept of the managerial "black box." Using it, we can characterize performance by *output measures* and *internal measures*. The first represent the output of the black box, and include such things as completing designs, meeting sales quotas, or increasing the yield in a production process—things we can and should plot on charts. The internal measures take into account activities that go on inside the black box: whatever is being done to create output for the period under review and also that which sets the stage for the output of future periods. Are we reaching our current production goals in such a way that two months from now we are likely to face a group of disgruntled production employees? Are we positioning and developing people in the organization in such a way that our business can handle its tasks in the future? Are we doing all of the things that add up to a well-run department? There is no strict formula by which we can compare the relative significance of output measures and internal measures. In a given situation, the proper weighting could be 50/50, 90/10, or 10/90 and could even shift from one month to the next. But at least we should know which two variables are being traded off against each other.

A similar kind of trade-off also has to be considered here: weighing long-term-oriented against short-term-oriented performance. An engineer working on the design of a product needs to complete the project on a strict schedule to generate revenue. He may also be working on a design *method* that will make it easier for others to design similar products in the future. The engineer obviously needs both activities evaluated and reviewed. Which is more significant? A way to help weigh questions like this is the idea of "present value" used in finance: how much will the future-oriented activity pay back over time? And how much is that worth today?

There is also a time factor to consider. The subordinate's output during the review period may have all, some, or nothing to do with his activities during the same period. Accordingly, the supervisor should look at the time offset between the activity of the subordinate and the output that results from that activity. Let me explain what I mean, because this is one lesson I learned the hard way. The organization of one of the managers reporting to me had had a superb year. All output measures were excellent, sales increased, profit margins were good, the products worked—you could hardly even think of giving anything but a superior review to the person in charge. Yet I had some misgivings. Turnover in his group was higher than it should have been, and his people were grumbling too much. There were other such straws in the wind, but who could give credence to elusive signs when tangible, measurable performance was so outstanding? So the manager got a very positive review.

The next year his organization took a nose dive. Sales growth disappeared, profitability declined, product development was delayed, and the turmoil among his subordinates deepened. As I prepared the next review of this manager, I struggled to sort out what had happened. Did the manager's performance deteriorate as suddenly as his organization's output measures indicated? What was going on? I concluded that in fact the manager's performance was improving in the second year, even as things seemed to go to hell. The problem was that his performance had not been good a year earlier. The output indicators merely represented work done years ago— the light from distant stars, as it were—which was still holding up. The time offset between the manager's work and the output of his organization was just about a year. Greatly embarrassed, I regretfully concluded that the superior rating I had given him was totally wrong. Trusting the internal measures, I should have had the judgment and courage to give the manager a much lower rating than I did in spite of the excellent output indicators that did not reflect the year under review.

The time offset between activity and output can also work the other way around. In the early years of Intel, I was called upon to review the performance of a subordinate who was setting up a production facility from scratch. It had not manufactured anything as yet, but of course the review could not wait for tangible output. I had had no prior experience supervising someone who did not have a record of concrete output. Here I gave my subordinate credit for doing well, even though output remained uncertain. As managers, we are really called upon to *judge* performance, not just to see and record it when it's in plain sight.

Finally, as you review a manager, should you be judging his performance or the performance of the group under his supervision? You should be doing both. Ultimately what you are after is the performance of the group, but the manager is there to *add value* in some way. You need to determine what that is. You must ask: Is he doing anything with his group? Is he hiring new people? Is he training the people he has, and doing other things that are likely to improve the output of the team in the future? The most difficult issues in determining a professional's performance will be based on asking questions and making judgments of this sort.

One big pitfall to be avoided is the "potential trap." At all times you should force yourself to assess performance, not potential. By "potential" I mean form rather than substance. I was once asked to approve the performance review of a general manager whose supervisor rated him highly for the year. The manager was responsible for a business unit that lost money, missed its revenue forecast month after month, slipped engineering schedules, and in general showed poor output and internal measures over the year. Accordingly, I could not approve the review. Whereupon his supervisor said, "But he is an outstanding general manager. He is knowledgeable and handles himself well. It's his organization that did not do well, not the manager himself!" This cut no ice with me because *the performance rating of a manager cannot be higher than the one we would accord to his organization!* It is very important to assess actual performance, not appearances; real output, not good form. Had the manager been given a high rating, Intel would have signaled to all at the company that to do well, you must "act" like a good manager, talk like one, and emulate one—but you don't need to perform like one.

A decision to promote is often linked, as it should be, to the performance review. We must recognize that no action communicates a manager's values to an organization more clearly and loudly than his choice of whom he promotes. By elevating someone, we are, in effect, creating role models for others in our organization. The old saying has it that when we promote our best salesman and make him a manager, we ruin a good salesman and get a bad manager. But if we think about it, we see we have no choice but to promote the good salesman. Should our worst salesman get the job? When we promote our best, we are saying to our subordinates that performance is what counts.

It is hard enough for us to assess our subordinates' performance, but we must also try to *improve* it. No matter how well a subordinate has done his job, we can always find ways to suggest improvement, something about which a manager need not feel embarrassed. Blessed with 20/20 hindsight, we can compare what the subordinate did against what he might have done, and the variance can tell both of us how to do things better in the future.

Delivering the Assessment

There are three L's to keep in mind when delivering a review: Level, listen, and leave yourself out.

You must level with your subordinate—the credibility and integrity of the entire system depend on your being totally frank. And don't be surprised to find that praising someone in a straightforward fashion can be just as hard as criticizing him without embarrassment.

The word "listen" has special meaning here. The aim

of communication is to transmit thoughts from the brain of person A to the brain of person B. Thoughts in the head of A are first converted into words, which are enunciated and via sound waves reach the ear of B; as nerve impulses they travel to his brain, where they are transformed back into thoughts and presumably kept. Should person A use a tape recorder to confirm the words used in the review? The answer is an emphatic no. Words themselves are nothing but a means; getting the right thought communicated is the end. Perhaps B has become so emotional that he can't understand something that would be perfectly clear to anyone else. Perhaps B has become so preoccupied trying to formulate answers that he can't really listen and get A's message. Perhaps B has tuned out and as a defense is thinking of going fishing. All of these possibilities can and do occur, and all the more so when A's message is laden with conflict.

How then can you be sure you are being truly heard? What techniques can you employ? Is it enough to have your subordinate paraphrase your words? I don't think so. What you must do is employ *all* of your sensory capabilities. To make sure you're being heard, you should *watch* the person you are talking to. Remember, the more complex the issue, the more prone communication is to being lost. Does your subordinate give appropriate responses to what you are saying? Does he allow himself to receive your message? If his responses —verbal and nonverbal—do not completely assure you that what you've said has gotten through, it is *your responsibility* to keep at it until you are satisfied that you have been heard and understood.

This is what I mean by *listening:* employing your entire arsenal of sensory capabilities to make certain your points are being properly interpreted by your subordinate's brain. All the intelligence and good faith used to prepare your review will produce nothing unless this occurs. Your tool, to say it again, is total listening.

Every good classroom teacher works in the same way. He knows when what he is saying is being understood by his students. If it isn't, he takes heed and explains things again or explains things in a different way. All of us have had professors who lectured by looking at the blackboard, mumbling to it, and carefully avoiding direct eye contact with the class. The reason: knowing that their presentation was murky and incomprehensible, these teachers looked away from their audience to avoid confirming visually what they already knew. So don't imitate your worst professors while delivering performance reviews. Listen with all your might to make sure your subordinate is receiving your message, and don't stop delivering it until you are satisfied that he is.

The third L is "leave yourself out." It is very important for you to understand that the performance review is about and for your subordinate. So your own insecurities, anxieties, guilt, or whatever should be kept out of it. At issue are the subordinate's problems, not the supervisor's, and it is the subordinate's day in court. Anyone called upon to assess the performance of another person is likely to have strong emotions before and during the review, just as actors have stage fright. You should work to control these emotions so that they don't affect your task, though they will well up no matter how many reviews you've given.

Let us now consider three types of performance reviews.

"On the One Hand . . . On the Other Hand . . ."

Most reviews probably fall into this category, containing both positive and negative assessments. Common problems here include superficiality, clichés, and laundry lists of unrelated observations. All of these will leave your subordinate bewildered and will hardly improve his future performance, the review's basic purpose. Let me suggest some ways to help you deliver this type of review.

The key is to recognize that your subordinate, like most people, has only a *finite capacity* to deal with facts, issues, and suggestions. You may possess seven truths about his performance, but if his capacity is only four, at best you'll waste your breath on the other three. At worst you will have left him with a case of sensory overload, and he will go away without getting anything out of the review. The fact is that a person can only absorb so many messages at one time, especially when they deal with his own performance. The purpose of the review is not to cleanse *your* system of all the truths you may have observed about your subordinate, but to improve *his* performance. So here less may very well be more.

How can you target a few key areas? First, consider as many aspects of your subordinate's performance as possible. You should scan material such as progress reports, performance against quarterly objectives, and one-on-one meeting notes. Then sit down with a blank piece of paper. As you consider your subordinate's performance, write everything down on the paper. Do *not* edit in your head. Get everything down, knowing that doing so doesn't commit you to do anything. Things major, minor, and trivial can be included in no particular order. When you have run out of items, you can put all of your supporting documentation away.

Now, from your worksheet, look for relationships between the various items listed. You will probably begin to notice that certain items are different manifestations of the same phenomenon, and that there may be some indications *why* a certain strength or weakness exists. When you find such relationships, you can start calling them "messages" for the subordinate. At this point, your worksheet might look something like that shown on the next page. Now, again from your worksheet, begin to

draw conclusions and specific examples to support them.
Once your list of messages has been compiled, ask yourself if your subordinate will be able to *remember* all of the
messages you have chosen to deliver. If not, you must
delete the less important ones. Remember, what you
couldn't include in this review, you can probably take up
in the next one.

POSITIVES	NEGATIVES
— planning process much better! (quick start)	— spec process: zero!
— good report to Materials Council	— debating society meetings—all mushy
— helped on Purchasing cost analysis project	— poor kick-off for spec training
	— confused on computer use
	— doesn't listen to peers (e.g. manufacturing groups)

Messages

1. Good results on planning system (analytical/financial background useful)
2. Hard time setting clear, crisp goals—satisfied with activities
instead of driving results!
3. Computer knowledge (No—let's just concentrate on #2!)

Worksheet for performance review.

Let's talk about surprises. If you have discharged
your supervisory responsibilities adequately throughout the year, holding regular one-on-one meetings and
providing guidance when needed, there should never
be any surprises at a performance review, right?
Wrong. When you are using the worksheet, sometimes

you come up with a message that will startle you. So
what do you do? You're faced with either delivering the
message or not, but if the purpose of the review is to
improve your subordinate's performance, you must deliver it. Preferably, a review should not contain any surprises, but if you uncover one, swallow hard and bring
it up.

On pages 200–201 you'll find an "on the one hand, on
the other hand" kind of performance review. It was written to correspond to the worksheet shown opposite. I
have annotated it to call attention to some of the things
we discussed in this chapter.

The Blast

With a little soul-searching, you may come to realize
that you have a major performance problem on your
hands. You have a subordinate who, unless turned
around, could get fired. To deal with the problem, you
and your subordinate will likely go through stages commonly experienced in problem-solving of all kinds and
particularly in conflict resolution. These are shown on
page 194. You'll find these occurring definitely during
and possibly after the "blast" review, which is basically
an exercise of resolving conflict about a big performance problem.

A poor performer has a strong tendency to *ignore* his
problem. Here a manager needs facts and examples so
that he can demonstrate its reality. Progress of some sort
is made when the subordinate *actively denies* the existence
of a problem rather than ignoring it passively, as before.
Evidence can overcome resistance here as well, and we
enter the third stage, when the subordinate admits that
there is a problem, but maintains it is not *his* problem.
Instead he will *blame others*, a standard defense mechanism. Using this defense, he can continue to avoid the
responsibility and burden of remedying the situation.

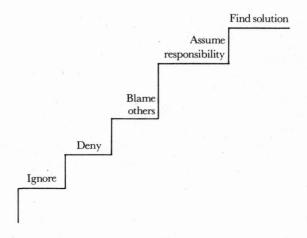

The stages of problem-solving: The transition from blaming others to assuming responsibility is an emotional step.

These three steps usually follow one another in fairly rapid succession. But things tend to get stuck at the blame-others stage. If your subordinate does have a problem, there's no way of resolving it if he continues to blame it on others. He has to take the biggest step: namely *assuming responsibility*. He has to say not only that there is a problem but that it is *his* problem. This is fateful, because it means work: "If it is my problem, I have to do something about it. If I have to do something, it is likely to be unpleasant and will definitely mean a lot of work on my part." Once responsibility has been assumed, however, *finding the solution* is relatively easy. This is because the move from blaming others to assuming responsibility constitutes an emotional step, while the move from assuming responsibility to finding the solution is an intellectual one, and the latter is easier.

It is the reviewer's job to get the subordinate to move through all of the stages to that of assuming responsibility, though finding the solution should be a shared task.

The supervisor should keep track of what stage things are in. If the supervisor wants to go on to find the solution when the subordinate is still denying or blaming others, nothing can happen. Knowing where you are will help you both move through the stages *together*.

In the end, there are three possible outcomes. One, the subordinate accepts your assessment and your recommended cure, and commits himself to take it. Two, he may disagree completely with your assessment but still accepts your cure. Three, the subordinate disagrees with your assessment and does *not* commit himself to do what you've recommended. As the supervisor, which of these three should you consider *acceptable* resolutions to the problem?

I feel very strongly that any outcome that includes a *commitment* to action is acceptable. Complex issues do not lend themselves easily to universal agreement. If your subordinate says he's committed to change things, you have to assume he's sincere. The key word here is *acceptable*. It is certainly more *desirable* for you and your subordinate to agree about the problem and the solution, because that will make you feel that he will enthusiastically work toward remedying it. So up to a point you should try to get your subordinate to agree with you. But if you can't, accept his commitment to change and go on. Don't confuse emotional comfort with operational need. To make things work, people do not need to side with you; you only need them to commit themselves to pursue a course of action that has been decided upon. There seems to be something not quite nice about expecting a person to walk down a path he'd rather not be on. But on the job we are after a person's performance, not our psychological comfort.

I learned the distinction between the two during one of the first reviews I had to give. I was trying very hard to persuade my subordinate to see things my way. He simply would not go along with me and finally said to me, "Andy, you will never convince me, but why do you insist on wanting to convince me? I've already said I will do what you say." I shut up, embarrassed, not knowing why. It took me a long time before I realized I was embarrassed because my insistence had a lot to do with making me feel better and little to do with the running of the business.

If it becomes clear that you are not going to get your subordinate past the blame-others stage, you will have to assume the formal role of the supervisor, endowed with position power, and say, "This is what I, as your boss, am instructing you to do. I understand that you do not see it my way. You may be right or I may be right. But I am not only empowered, I am required by the organization for which we both work to give you instructions, and this is what I want you to do . . ." And proceed to secure your subordinate's *commitment* to the course of action you want and thereafter monitor his *performance* against that commitment.

Recently one of my subordinates wrote a review that I considered superficial, lacking analysis and depth. My subordinate, after some discussion, agreed with my assessment, but he considered the issue not important enough, as he put it, to spend time rewriting the review. After more spirited discussion, we remained deadlocked. Finally, I took a deep breath and said to him, "Look, I understand that you don't consider it worth your time to do it. But I *want* you to do it." I added that "I guess there is a basic difference between us. The integrity of the performance review system is just more important to me than it is to you. That is why I have to insist." He looked back at me and after a moment simply said, "Okay." He thought I was out in left field and resented the fact that I made him spend time on something he thought was unimportant, but he committed himself to redo the review, and, in fact, he did it well. His subordinate ended up getting the reworked, much more thorough and thoughtful review, and the fact that his review was rewritten without the agreement of *my* subordinate made no difference to him.

Reviewing the Ace

After trying to establish the principles of performance appraisal with a group of about twenty middle managers, I asked them to take a review they had once received and to analyze it according to our new criteria. The results were not what I expected, but I did learn from them.

This group consisted of achievers, and their ratings were mostly very high. The reviews were exceptionally well written, much better than the average at Intel. However, for content, they tended to be retrospective assessments, analyses of what the subordinate had done in the course of the prior year. Even though their key purpose was to improve the subordinate's future performance, a majority of the reviews made little or no attempt to define what the subordinate needed to do to improve his performance or even to maintain his current level. It seems that for an achiever the supervisor's effort goes into determining and justifying the judgment of the superior performance, while giving little attention to how he could do even better. But for a poor performer, the supervisor tends to concentrate heavily on ways he can improve performance, providing detailed and elaborate "corrective action programs," step-by-step affairs meant to ensure that the marginal employee can pull himself up to meet minimum requirements.

I think we have our priorities reversed. Shouldn't we spend more time trying to improve the performance of our stars? After all, these people account for a disproportionately large share of the work in any organization. Put another way, concentrating on the stars is a high- ✔ leverage activity: if they get better, the impact on group output is very great indeed.

We all have a hard time saying things that are critical,

whether we're talking to a superior employee or a marginal one. We must keep in mind, however, that no matter how stellar a person's performance level is, there is *always* room for improvement. Don't hesitate to use the 20/20 hindsight provided by the review to show anyone, even an ace, how he might have done better.

Other Thoughts and Practices

Is it a good idea to ask the subordinate to prepare some kind of a *self-review* before being reviewed by his supervisor? Let me answer the question this way. Your own review is obviously important to you, and you really want to know how your supervisor sees your year's work. If you prepare a review and give it to your supervisor, and he simply changes the format, retypes it, gives you a superior rating, and then hands it back to you, how will you feel? Probably cheated. If you have to tell your supervisor about your accomplishments, he obviously doesn't pay much attention to what you are doing. Reviewing the performance of subordinates is a formal act of leadership. If supervisors permit themselves to be prompted in one way or another, their leadership and their capacity for it will begin to appear false. So the integrity of the supervisors' judgment here must be preserved at all costs, and they must commit themselves through an up-front judgment of their subordinates' performance if the health and vitality of the review process are to be maintained.

What about asking your subordinate to evaluate *your* performance as his supervisor? I think this might be a good idea. But you should make it clear to your subordinate that it's your job to assess his performance, while his assessment of you has only advisory status. The point is, he is not your leader; you are his. And under no circumstances should you pretend that you and your subordinates are equal during performance reviews.

Should you deliver the written review before, during, or after the face-to-face discussion? I have tried it all three ways. Let's consider some of the pros and cons of each. What happens if you have the review first and then give your subordinate what you've written later? Upon reading it, the subordinate may find a phrase that he didn't "hear" earlier and blow up over it. What about delivering the written review *during* the discussion? One manager told me that he gives the subordinate a copy of the review and tells him to read the first several paragraphs, which they then discuss. Grouping the paragraphs, supervisor and subordinate work their way through the appraisal. I can see a problem with this. How can a supervisor ask a subordinate to stop at paragraph three when he is so eager to read the rest of what he's got? Another manager told me that he reads the written review to his subordinate to try to control the session. But here, too, the subordinate is left eager to know what comes next and might not pay attention to what is really being said. Also, when your subordinate is given a written review during the discussion, he won't have the time to think about what it says and is likely to walk away muttering to himself, "I should have said this in response, and I should have said that." For a good meeting of minds, your subordinate should have time to work out his reactions to what's in the review.

In my experience, the best thing to do is to give your subordinate the written review sometime *before* the face-to-face discussion. He can then read the whole thing privately and digest it. He can react or overreact and then look at the "messages" again. By the time the two of you get together, he will be much more prepared, both emotionally and rationally.

Preparing and delivering a performance assessment is one of the hardest tasks you'll have to perform as a manager. The best way to learn how to do one is to think critically about the reviews you yourself have received.

EXEMPT PERFORMANCE APPRAISAL

NAME __John Doe__ JOB TITLE __Materials Support Supervisor__

REVIEW PERIOD _____ 2/82 _____ TO _____ 8/82 _____

DESCRIPTION OF JOB ASSIGNMENT:

Responsible for managing the production planning process and the manufacturing specifications process, including maintenance and development.

ACCOMPLISHMENTS DURING THIS REVIEW PERIOD:

Output measure: good ➤ The production planning process was significantly changed this year. Sites were well coordinated, and all the administrative activities were efficiently done.

EVALUATION: (AREAS OF STRENGTHS, AREAS FOR IMPROVEMENTS)

John transferred to Materials Support in early February. The production planning process was in some difficulties at the time he joined the group. John got up to speed very quickly and was able to take over the job from his predecessor very effectively.

In the manufacturing specifications area, John's efforts have been far less successful to date. John puts effort into these areas, but the results have not been satisfactory. I think that the problem has two causes.

Internal measure: lacking; activity vs. output ➤ —John has a hard time defining clear, concise, and specific goals. A clear example of this is his difficulty setting good objectives and key results. Another example is the mushy conclusion of the manufacturing specification system review in March. We still don't have a clear definitive statement of where the spec system is heading and how it is going to get there. Without specific goals, one can very easily fall into the trap of "working on" things without reaching the objectives—which leads to the second issue.

Note: statement supported by example ➤ —I feel that John is easily satisfied that having a meeting on a subject constitutes progress. This happened, for example, in the area of training associated with manufacturing specs. John should spend more effort prior to each meeting and define what specific results he wants to accomplish with it.

Compliments need examples, too! →

John's prior finance background has really helped in a variety of work areas. For example, John voluntarily helped the Purchasing group sort out some of their finance problems—an effort over and above the call of duty.

John would like to be promoted to the next management level. This will not happen at this time, but I am satisfied that his capabilities will allow him to eventually be promoted. Before that happens, however, John has to be able to take complex projects, like the manufacturing spec system, and show <u>results</u>. This will require clear and concise breakdown of problems, identification of

Attempt to show <u>how</u> to improve performance →

goals, and establishment of the way to achieve those goals. John, for the most part, will have to achieve this on his own. While I will help when needed, John has to be the primary driver. Only when he shows that he is capable of independent work along these lines can he be promoted.

In summary, John is capable of doing his current job. I also realize the difficulty John has had in changing from the finance environment to a manufacturing environment. I will continue to try to help him—particularly in the areas of goal setting and defining ways of accomplishing his tasks. John's performance in Materials Support is rated as "meets requirements"—a rating he should definitely be able to improve.

RATING: ☐ DOES NOT   ☐ MEETS
                 MEET   REQUIREMENTS
                 REQUIREMENTS
                          ☐ EXCEEDS
                            REQUIREMENTS
☐ SUPERIOR

Two levels of management plus personnel required, for checks and balances

IMMEDIATE SUPERVISOR: *GAW*   DATE: 8/10/82
APPROVING SUPERVISOR: *DAF*   DATE: 8/15/82
MATRIX MANAGER: *ECM*   DATE: 8/10/82
PERSONNEL ADMINISTRATOR: *RMM*   DATE: 8/18/82
EMPLOYEE: *John Doe*   DATE: 8/22/82

Note: Review was prepared jointly with head of the Material Manager's Council: an example of dual reporting

Employee signature shows that he has been given the review; does not necessarily mean he agrees with it

And if you've been lucky, the tradition of good performance reviews has been handed from supervisor to subordinate, which has helped to maintain the integrity of the system in your company. Nevertheless, people constantly need to be prodded into doing a good job of reviewing. Each year I read something like a hundred evaluations, all of those written by my own subordinates and a random selection from throughout Intel. I comment on them and send them back for rewrites or with a complimentary note. I do this with as much noise and visibility as I can, because I want to reiterate and reaffirm the significance the system has and should have for every Intel employee. Anything less would not be appropriate for the most important kind of task-relevant feedback we can give our subordinates.

14
Two Difficult Tasks

There are two other emotionally charged tasks a manager must perform. They are interviewing a potential employee and trying to talk a valued employee out of quitting.

Interviewing

The purpose of the interview is to:

- select a good performer
- educate him as to who you and the company are
- determine if a mutual match exists
- sell him on the job

The means at your disposal typically consist of an hour or two of interview time and a check of the candidate's references. We know how hard it is to assess the actual past performance of our own subordinates even though we spent much time working closely with them. Here we sit somebody down and try to find out in an hour how well he is likely to perform in an entirely new environment. If performance appraisal is difficult, interviewing is just about impossible. The fact is, we managers have no choice but to perform the interview, no matter how hard it is. But we must realize that the risks of failure are high.

The other tool we have for assessing potential performance is to research past performance by checking references. But you'll often be talking to a total stranger, so even if he comments freely about the candidate, what he says won't have much meaning to you without some knowledge of how his company does business and what values it works by. Moreover, while few references will out-and-out lie, they tend not to volunteer specific critical remarks. So reference-checking hardly exempts you from getting as much as you can out of the interview.

CONDUCTING THE INTERVIEW

The applicant should do 80 percent of the talking during the interview, and *what* he talks about should be your main concern. But you have a great deal of control here by being an active listener. Keep in mind you only have an hour or so to listen. When you ask a question, a garrulous or nervous person might go on and on with his answer long after you've lost interest. Most of us will sit and listen until the end out of courtesy. Instead, you should interrupt and stop him, because if you don't, you are wasting your only asset—the interview time, in which you have to get as much information and insight as possible. So when things go off the track, get them back on quickly. Apologize if you like, and say, "I would like to change the subject to X, Y, or Z." The interview is yours to control, and if you don't, you have only yourself to blame.

An interview produces the most insight if you steer the discussion toward subjects familiar to both you and the candidate. The person should talk about himself, his experience, what he has done and why, what he would have done differently if he had it to do over, and so forth, but this should be done in terms familiar to you, so that you can evaluate its significance. In short, make sure the words used mean the same thing to both of you.

What are the subjects that you should bring up during an interview? A group of managers provided me with what they thought were the best questions. They were:

— Describe some projects that were highly regarded by your management, especially by the levels above your immediate supervisor.
— What are your weaknesses? How are you working to eliminate them?
— Convince me why my company should hire you.
— What are some of the problems you are encountering in your current position? How are you going about solving them? What could you have done to prevent them from cropping up?
— Why do you think you're ready for this new job?
— What do you consider your most significant achievements? Why were they important to you?
— What do you consider your most significant failures? What did you learn from them?
— Why do you think an engineer should be chosen for a marketing position? (Vary this one according to the situation.)
— What was the most important course or project you completed in your college career? Why was it so important?

The information to be gained here tends to fall into four distinct categories. First, you're after an understanding of the candidate's *technical* knowledge: not engineering or scientific knowledge, but what he knows about performing the job he wants—his skill level. For an accountant, technical skill means an understanding of accounting; for a tax lawyer, tax laws; for an actuary, statistics and the use of actuarial tables; and so on. Second, you're trying to assess how this person performed in an earlier job *using* his skills and technical knowledge;

in short, not just what the candidate knows, but also what he *did* with what he knows. Third, you are after the reasons why there may be any *discrepancy* between what he knew and what he did, between his capabilities and his performance. And finally, you are trying to get a feel for his set of *operational values,* those that would guide him on the job.

Let's look at how the questions above fit into the four categories.

Technical/Skills
describe some projects
what are your weaknesses

What He Did With Knowledge
past achievements
past failures

Discrepancies
what did you learn from failures
problems in current position

Operational Values
why are you ready for new job
why should my company hire you
why should engineer be chosen for marketing
most important college course/project

The ultimate purpose of interviewing is to make a judgment about how the candidate would perform in your company's environment. This is at odds with a principle we stressed about performance reviews: the need to avoid the "potential" trap. But when you're hiring, you must judge potential contribution. Within the hour or so at your disposal, you must move between the world of the past employer and your own, and project the candidate's future performance in a new environment based on his own description of past performance. This managerial task is clearly tricky and high-risk, but unfortunately unavoidable.

You can't get away from relying on a candidate's self-assessment. But that's not a bad way to get direct answers to direct questions. If, for example, you were to ask, "How good are you technically?" the interviewee might be taken back momentarily but then clear his throat and say timidly, "Well, I think I'm pretty good . . ." As you listen, you'll probably get a decent fix on how capable he really is. Don't worry about being blunt; direct questions tend to bring direct answers, and when they don't, they produce other forms of insight into the candidate.

Asking a candidate to handle a hypothetical situation can also enlighten you. I once interviewed someone for the position of cost accountant at Intel. He had a Harvard MBA and came from the food service industry. He knew nothing about the semiconductor business and I knew nothing about finance, so we really couldn't talk in much detail about his technical ability to do the job. I decided to take him through the semiconductor manufacturing process step by step. After saying I would answer any specific questions he had, I asked him what the finished cost of a wafer would be. He asked some questions and pondered matters for a while. He then started to think his way through the basic semiconductor cost accounting principles, discovering some of them as he went along, and ultimately came up with the correct answer. He was hired, because this exercise demonstrated (as it turns out, correctly) that his problem-solving capacity was first-rate.

Another approach follows that you may want to use while interviewing. The candidate can tell you a great deal about his capabilities, skills, and values by asking *you* questions. Ask the candidate what he would like to know about you, the company, or the job. The questions he asks will tell you what he already knows about the company, what he would like to know more about, and how well prepared he is for the interview. There's nothing foolproof about this, however. Once a prospective manager came to my office with a copy of our annual report, which he had read very carefully and marked up with penetrating questions. In fact, I couldn't answer many of them. I was very impressed. We hired him and he failed badly on the job. As I said, interviewing is a high-risk proposition . . .

A final point about references: when you are talking to them, you're really after the same information that you tried to get directly from the candidate. If you know the reference personally, you have a much better chance of getting "real" information. If you don't, try to keep him on the phone long enough to let some sort of personal bond develop. If you can uncover some common experience or association, the reference will probably become more open with you. In my experience, the last ten minutes of a half-hour conversation are much more valuable than the first ten minutes, thanks to that bond.

If possible, you should talk with the applicant again after you have checked his references, because you may have gotten some new perspectives. Such a follow-up interview can be quite a focused affair.

What about "tricks"? The best ones I've heard about come to me from somebody who had tried to get into the Navy's nuclear submarine program. Admiral Rickover apparently personally interviewed each candidate and employed techniques like having the candidate sit on a three-legged chair. When it tipped over, the poor man would be left sprawling on the floor. Rickover evidently thought the trick tested strength of character in the face of embarrassment. But I think the interview should be completely straightforward. Remember, a candidate is a potential employee. He will go away from having talked to you with a strong set of first impressions. If those are wrong and you hire the person, it will take a long time before they change. So show yourself and your environment as they really are.

Are there any guarantees of success? Several years ago I interviewed a person for a high-level position at Intel. I did the work as carefully and thoroughly as I could. I had a very good feel, I thought, of the whys and wherefores of the person's skills, past performance, and values, and we hired him. From day one he was a disaster. Much humbled, I've since gone over my notes from the interviews and the conversations with references. To this day I haven't a clue about why I didn't spot the candidate's considerable flaws. So in the end careful interviewing doesn't guarantee you anything, it merely increases your odds of getting lucky.

"I Quit!"

This is what I most dread as a manager: a subordinate, highly valued and esteemed, decides to quit. I am talking not about someone whose motives are more money and better perks at another company, but about an employee who is dedicated and loyal yet feels his work is not appreciated. You and the company don't want to lose him, and his decision to leave reflects on you. If he feels his efforts have gone unrecognized, you have not done your job and have failed as his manager.

The opening shot usually occurs when you are on the run. On your way to what you consider an important meeting, your subordinate timidly stops you and mutters under his breath, "Do you have a minute?" He then mutters further that he has decided to leave the company. You look at him wide-eyed. *Your initial reaction to his announcement is absolutely crucial.* If you're human, you'll probably want to escape to your meeting, and you mumble something back about talking things over later. But in almost all such cases, the employee is quitting because he feels he is not important to you. If you do not deal with the situation right at the first mention, you'll confirm his feelings and the outcome is inevitable.

Drop what you are doing. Sit him down and ask him *why* he is quitting. Let him talk—don't argue about anything with him. Believe me, he's rehearsed his speech countless times during more than one sleepless night. After he's finished going through all his reasons for wanting to leave (they won't be good ones), ask him more questions. Make *him* talk, because after the prepared points are delivered, the real issues may come out. Don't argue, don't lecture, and don't panic. Remember, this is only the opening skirmish, not the war. And you cannot win the war here—but you can lose it! You have to convey to him *by what you do* that he is important to you, and you have to find out what is really troubling him. Don't try to change his mind at this point, but buy time. After he's said all he has to say, ask for whatever time you feel is necessary to prepare yourself for the next round. But know that you must follow through on whatever you've committed yourself to do.

What's your next move? Because you have a major problem, you go to your supervisor for help and advice. He no doubt is also on his way to an important meeting . . . He, like you, will try to put things off, and most probably not because he doesn't care, but because the situation affects you more than your supervisor—after all, it is *your* subordinate who has decided to quit. It is up to you to make it your supervisor's problem and make him participate in the solution to your problem.

Corporate citizenship will probably play a substantial role in what happens next. Your subordinate is a valued employee—of the company. You now must vigorously pursue every avenue available to you to keep him with the firm, even if it means transferring him to another department. If it seems that is the likely solution, you must become the project manager of that solution until the whole thing is settled. You may ask why you should put yourself out to keep an employee whom you are going to lose. There is a basic principle involved: you owe it to your employer to save an employee for the company. Beyond this, the golden rule can become more than a nice ideal in situations of this sort. Today you save a valued contributor for the company by virtually giving him to a fellow manager. Tomorrow it will be his turn to do you the same favor. In the long run, if all managers take this position, they will all win.

Now you may be ready to go back to your subordinate with a solution, one that addresses his real reasons for wanting to quit and one that in turn will benefit the company. By now he should know that he is important to you, but he might say that you should have offered him the new position long ago. He might go on to say that you're only doing it now because he *forced* you into it, his feeling being that "If I stay, you'll think of me as the blackmailer forever!"

You now have to make him feel comfortable with the new arrangement. You might say something like, "You did not blackmail us into doing anything we shouldn't have done anyway. When you almost quit, you shook us up and made us aware of the error of our ways. We are just doing what we should have done without any of this happening."

Then your subordinate may say he's accepted a job somewhere else and can't back out. You have to make him quit again. You say he's really made *two* commitments: first to a potential employer he only vaguely knows, and second to you, his present employer. And commitments he has made to the people he has been working with daily are far stronger than one made to a casual new acquaintance.

As I said, the whole thing is not easy, either for the subordinate or the supervisor. But you must give it your best shot, because the good of the company is involved and the issue is even more important than keeping one valued employee. This subordinate is valuable and important because he has attributes that make him so. Other employees respect him; and if they are like him, they identify with him. So other superior performers like him will track what happens to him, and their morale and commitment to the company will hinge on the outcome of this person's fate.

15

Compensation as Task-Relevant Feedback

Money has significance at all levels of Maslow's motivation hierarchy. As noted earlier, a person needs money to buy food, housing, and insurance policies, which are part of his physiological and safety/security needs. As one moves up the need hierarchy, money begins to mean something else—a measure of one's worth in a competitive environment. Earlier I described a simple test that can be applied to determine the role money plays for someone. If the *absolute* amount of a raise in salary is important, that person is probably motivated by physiological or safety/security needs. If the *relative* amount of a raise—what he got compared to others—is the important issue, that person is likely to be motivated by self-actualization, because money here is a measure, not a necessity.

At higher levels of compensation, an incremental amount of money gradually will have less and less material utility to the person who gets it. In my experience, middle managers are usually paid well enough that money does not have crucial material significance to them, but not well enough that it is without any material significance. Of course, one middle manager's needs can differ greatly from another's, depending on individual circumstances—number of children, a working spouse or not, and so on. As a supervisor, you have to be very sensitive toward the various money needs of your subordinates and show empathy toward them. You must be especially careful not to project your own circumstances onto others.

As managers, our concern is to get a high level of performance from our subordinates. So we want to dispense, allocate, and use money as a way to deliver *task-relevant feedback*. To do this, compensation should obviously be tied to performance, but that, as we've seen, is very hard to assess precisely. Because a middle manager cannot be paid by the piece, his job can never be defined by simple output. And because his performance is woven into the performance of a team, it is hard to design a compensation scheme tied directly to the individual performance of a middle manager.

But compromises can be set up. We can base a *portion* of a middle manager's compensation on his performance. Let's call this a *performance bonus*. The percentage the bonus represents of a manager's total compensation should rise with his total compensation. Thus, for a highly paid senior manager, for whom the absolute dollars make relatively little difference, the performance bonus should be as high as 50 percent, while a middle manager should receive more in the range of 10 to 25 percent of his total compensation this way. Even though what he makes is typically at a level where substantial fluctuations could cause personal hardship, we can at least give a taste of task-relevant feedback.

To design a good performance bonus scheme, we must deal with a variety of issues. We need to figure out if the performance is linked to a team or if it is mostly related to individual work. If it is the former, who makes up the team? Is it a project team, a division, or the entire corporation? We also need to figure out what period the performance bonus should cover, realizing again that cause and effect tend to be offset from each other, often by a long time, but a bonus needs to be paid close enough to the time the work was done that the subordinate can remember why it was awarded. Furthermore, we must think about whether the bonus should be based strictly on countable items (financial performance, for example), on achieving measurable objectives, or on some subjective elements that might get us drawn into a beauty contest. Finally, of course, we don't want to devise something that pays out lavishly even as the company is going bankrupt.

If you take all of this into account, you are likely to come up with some complex arrangements. For example, you might have a scheme in which a manager's performance bonus is based on three factors. The first would include his individual performance only, as judged by his supervisor. The second would account for his immediate team's objective performance, his department perhaps. The third factor would be linked to the overall financial performance of the corporation. When you take, let's say, 20 percent of a manager's compensation and split it into three parts, any one will have only a small impact on total compensation, yet attention will still be called to its significance. No matter what way you choose to determine bonuses, none gives you exactly what you want, but most of them will spotlight performance and deliver task-relevant feedback.

Let's now look at the administration of base salaries. In the abstract, there are two ways to do it. At one extreme, the dollar level is determined by experience only; at the other, by merit alone. In the experience-only approach, an employee's salary increases with the time he has spent in a particular position. A key point here is that any job has a maximum value; no matter how long an individual has been in it, his salary ultimately has to level off, as shown in the figure on the next page. In the merit-only approach, salary is independent of the time spent in the job. Here the theory says, "I don't care if you are one year out of college or have spent twenty years in the work force. I only care to see how you perform in this

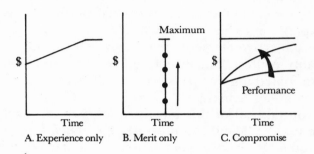

	A. Experience only	B. Merit only	C. Compromise

There are two pure forms of salary administration; most companies use a compromise.

job." But here too, of course, a given job still has a maximum value. Social norms can force us into some unfortunate compensation practices. For instance, even though we say that every job has a finite value where compensation should level off, we often let an individual become too highly paid because we, management, keep giving routine raises.

Many organizations practice a pure experience-only form of salary administration. Large Japanese companies tend to place no distinction based on performance during the first ten or so years of employment—which are probably the most productive years of a professional's life. Likewise, unions and most government jobs lean toward pure experience-only salary scales. Apart from whether this is fair or not, the message from management is that performance doesn't matter much. Consider teachers in many school systems. A good one gets paid the same salary as a bad one if they both have been around for the same length of time. How a teacher is evaluated is not usually tied even symbolically to compensation, which makes me wonder if the pass/fail system of grading did not have its origin in the way the typical teacher is paid.

At the same time, merit-only salary administration is impractical in its pure form. It is very hard to ignore a person's experience as you try to pay a fair salary. Thus, most companies choose a course between the two extremes, which is a compromise scheme that takes the shape of a family of curves shown in the previous figure. The shapes of all of them approximate the curve representing the experience-only approach, but as you can see, while people start at the same salary level, they move up at different speeds and arrive at different places, depending upon individual performance.

Of the three schemes, the one based on experience only is obviously the easiest to administer. If your subordinate does not like the raise he's been given, all you have to do is show him the book where it says that for X amount of time on the job he deserves and gets Y amount of pay. A supervisor trying to administer some type of merit-based or compromise scheme has to deal with the allocation of a finite resource—money—and this requires thought and effort. If we want to use such schemes, we have to come to terms with the principle— troubling to many managers—that any merit-based system requires a competitive, comparative evaluation of individuals.

Merit-based compensation simply cannot work unless we understand that if someone is going to be first, somebody else has to be last. As Americans, we have no problem accepting a competitive ranking in a sports event. Even the person who comes in last in a race feels comfortable about the system that says someone has to finish last. But at work, unfortunately, competitive ranking frequently becomes a highly charged issue, difficult to accept and to administer—yet it is a must if

we want to use salary as a way to encourage performance.

Promotions, defined as a substantial change in a person's job, are very important to the health of any organization and should be considered with great care. Obviously, for the individual concerned, promotions often
produce a big raise. As we have seen, promotions are
also readily seen by other members of the organization,
and so take on a vitally important role in communicating
a value system to the rest of the company. Promotions
must be based on performance, because that is the only
way to keep the idea of performance highlighted, maintained, and perpetuated.

If we are going to consider promotions, we have to
consider the Peter Principle, which says that when someone is good at his job, he is promoted; he keeps getting
promoted until he reaches his level of incompetence and
then stays there. Like all good caricatures, this one captures at least some of what really happens in a merit-
based promotion system.

Take a look at the illustration opposite, where we track
someone's promotions. At point A the demands of Job
1 so tax him that he can only perform in an average
fashion. In the jargon of performance assessment, he
"meets the requirements" of the job. As time passes, he
receives more training and becomes more motivated,
and improves his performance to an above-average level,
or, again in the jargon, to a point where he "exceeds the
requirements" of the position. At this time we consider
the person promotable, and in fact do promote him to
Job 2, where he will at first perform only at a "meets
requirements" level. With more experience, he again
will "exceed the requirements" of the job. Eventually, he
probably gets promoted again and the cycle repeats itself. Thus, an achiever will alternate between the "meets
requirements" and the "exceeds requirements" ratings
throughout his career, until he eventually settles at a

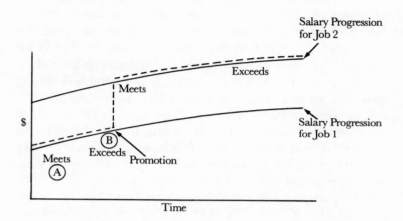

An achiever will alternate between "meets requirements" and "exceeds requirements" ratings throughout his career.

"meets requirements" level, at which time he will no longer be promoted. This, perhaps, is a better description of how the Peter Principle works.

Now, is there an alternative to this? I say there is not. If we take a person at point B and don't offer him more work and greater challenges even though he "exceeds the requirements" of Job 1, we are not fully utilizing a human resource of the company. In time, he will atrophy, and his performance will return to a "meets requirements" level and stay there.

Thus, you'll find two basic types of "meets" performers. One has no motivation to do more or faces no challenge to do more. This is the noncompetitor, who has become settled and satisfied in his job. The other type of "meets" performer is the competitor. Each time he reaches a level of "exceeds requirements," he becomes a candidate for promotion. Upon being promoted, he very likely becomes a "meets" performer again. This is the person Dr. Peter wrote about. But we really have no choice but to promote until a level of "incompetence" is reached. At least this way we drive our subordinates toward higher performance, and while they may perform at a "meets" level half the time, they will do that at an increasingly more challenging and difficult job level.

There are times when a person is promoted into a position so much over his head that he performs in a below-average fashion for too long a time. The solution is to *recycle* him: to put him back into the job he did well before he was promoted. Unfortunately, this is a very difficult thing to do in our society. People tend to view it as a personal failure. In fact, management was at fault for misjudging the employee's readiness for more responsibility. Usually the person who was promoted beyond his capability is forced to leave the company rather than encouraged to take a step back. This is often rationalized by the notion that "It is better that we let him go, for his own sake." I think it is dead wrong to force someone in such circumstances out of the company. Instead, I think management ought to face up to its own error in judgment and take forthright and deliberate steps to place the person into a job he can do. Management should also support the employee in the face of the embarrassment that he is likely to feel. If recycling is done openly, all will be pleasantly surprised how short-lived that embarrassment will be. And the result will be a person doing work we *know* from past experience he can perform well. In my experience, such people, once they regain their confidence, will be excellent candidates for another promotion at a later time—and the second time they are likely to succeed.

In sum, we managers must be responsible and provide our subordinates with honest performance ratings and honest merit-based compensation. If we do, the eventual result will be performance valued for its own sake throughout our organization.

One More Thing...

Please! You invested the price of this book plus perhaps eight hours of your time. At the risk of sounding like the author of a diet book, I would ask you to do something specific, and I leave you with a set of assignments. Choose what you like—but choose some—and perform them honestly.

You have trusted me enough to buy my book and read it. Now let me say a final thing: if you do at least 100 points worth of what you find here, you'll be a distinctly better manager for it.

Production	Points
Identify the operations in your work most like process, assembly, and test production.	10
For a project you are working on, identify the limiting step and map out the flow of work around it.	10
Define the proper places for the equivalents of receiving inspection, in-process inspection, and final inspection in your work. De-cide whether these inspections should be	

Points

monitoring steps or gate-like. Identify the
conditions under which you can relax things
and move to a variable inspection scheme.   10

Identify half a dozen new indicators for your
group's output. They should measure both
the quantity and quality of the output.   10

Install these new indicators as a routine in
your work area, and establish their regular
review in your staff meetings.   20

What is the most important strategy (plan of
action) you are pursing now? Describe the
environmental demand that prompted it and
your current status or momentum. Is your
strategy likely to result in a satisfactory state
of affairs for you or your organization if suc-
cessfully implemented?   20

Leverage

Conduct work simplification on your most te-
dious, time-consuming task. Eliminate at least
30 percent of the total number of steps involved.   10

Define your output: What are the output elements of the organization you manage and
the organizations you can influence? List
them in order of importance.   10

Analyze your information- and knowledge-
gathering system. Is it properly balanced
among "headlines," "newspaper articles,"
and "weekly news magazines"? Is redun-
dancy built in?   10

Take a "tour." Afterward, list the transactions you got involved in during its course.   10

Points

Create a once-a-month "excuse" for a tour.   10

Describe how you will monitor the next project you delegate to a subordinate. What will you look for? How? How frequently?   10

Generate an inventory of projects on which you can work at discretionary times.   10

Hold a scheduled one-on-one with each of your subordinates. (Explain to them in advance what a one-on-one is about. Have them prepare for it.)   20

Look at your calendar for the last week. Classify your activities as low-/medium-/high-leverage. Generate a plan of action to do more of the high-leverage category. (What activities will you reduce?)   10

Forecast the demand on your time for the next week. What portion of your time is likely to be spent in meetings? Which of these are process-oriented meetings? Mission-oriented meetings? If the latter are over 25 percent of your total time, what should you do to reduce them?   10

Define the three most important objectives for your organization for the next three months. Support them with key results.   20

Have your subordinates do the same for themselves, after a thorough discussion of the set generated above.   20

Generate an inventory of pending decisions you are responsible for. Take three and structure the decision-making process for them, using the six-question approach.   10

Performance	Points
Evaluate your own motivational state in terms of the Maslow hierarchy. Do the same for each of your subordinates.	10
Give your subordinates a racetrack: define a set of performance indicators for each.	20
List the various forms of task-relevant feedback your subordinates receive. How well can they gauge their progress through them?	10
Classify the task-relevant maturity of each of your subordinates as low, medium, or high. Evaluate the management style that would be most appropriate for each. Compare what your own style is with what it should be.	10
Evaluate the last performance review you received and also the last set of reviews you gave to your subordinates as a means of delivering task-relevant feedback. How well did the reviews do to improve performance? What was the nature of the communication process during the delivery of each?	20
Redo one of these reviews as it should have been done.	10

Notes

Business Review, vol. 53, no. 4, July–August 1975, pp. 49–61) that other managers' days are altogether similar to mine.

51 The idea of "nudging" as an important element of the decision-making process was pointed out by my colleague Les Vadasz.

4 MEETINGS—THE MEDIUM OF MANAGERIAL WORK

76 "The good time users . . .": Peter Drucker, *People and Performance: Peter Drucker on Management* (New York: Harper's College Press, 1977), p. 57.

5 DECISIONS, DECISIONS

90 "In the meeting . . .": Robert L. Simison, "Ford Fires an Economist," *Wall Street Journal,* July 30, 1980, p. 20.

93 This role-playing experiment, as well as the peer-group syndrome, was first suggested by Gerry Parker, a senior technologist at Intel.

98 The six-question approach to expedite the decision-making process was suggested by Les Vadasz of Intel.

101 "Group decisions . . .": Alfred P. Sloan, Jr., *My Years with General Motors* (New York: Doubleday, 1964), p. 512.

6 PLANNING

112 Columbus: To spread my guilt in tinkering with history, I hasten to credit my colleagues Harry Chapman and Rosemary Remacle for this adaptation.

PART III

8 HYBRID ORGANIZATIONS

123 "Good management . . .": Sloan, op. cit., p. 505.

9 DUAL REPORTING

131 Books have been written about matrix management: An example is Jay R. Galbraith, *Designing Complex Organizations* (Reading, Mass.: Addison-Wesley, 1973).

138   "A university is an odd place to manage. . . .": John A. Prestbo, "Pinching Pennies: Ohio University Finds Participatory Planning Ends Financial Chaos," *Wall Street Journal*, May 27, 1981, pp. 1, 20.

10 MODES OF CONTROL

145   the three means of control: Oliver E. Williamson, *Markets and Hierarchies: Analysis and Antitrust Implications* (New York: Free Press, 1975); Raymond L. Price and William G. Ouchi, "Hierarchies, Clans and Theory Z: A New Perspective on Organization Development," *Organizational Dynamics*, Autumn 1978, pp. 35–44.

PART IV

11 THE SPORTS ANALOGY

159   Maslow's theory: Abraham H. Maslow, *Motivation and Personality* (New York: Harper & Row, 1954).

169   "It astounds Joe Frazier . . .": "Fight One More Round," *Time*, December 14, 1981, p. 90.

170   "thrived on beating the competition . . .": Bundsen, syndicated column, *Peninsula Times Tribune* (Palo Alto, Calif.), September 18, 1982, p. B-3C.

12 TASK-RELEVANT MATURITY

173   For a compilation of work on task-relevant maturity, see Paul Hersey and Kenneth H. Blanchard, *Management of Organizational Behavior*, 2nd. ed. (New York: Prentice-Hall, 1972).

Index

About the Author

Born in Hungary, ANDREW S. GROVE left in the aftermath of the 1956 revolution. Three years later he graduated first in his class from the City College of New York with a degree in chemical engineering. After three more years he obtained a Ph.D. from the University of California at Berkeley.

As a scientist, Grove participated in bringing about major breakthroughs in the technology of semiconductors. As an entrepreneur, he helped found Intel Corporation, which he now serves as president. Grove, a recipient of the Certificate of Merit from the Franklin Institute and a member of the National Academy of Engineering, is also the author of the widely used text *Physics and Technology of Semiconductor Devices*.

Grove lives with his wife and two daughters on the San Francisco peninsula.